In-Between

Bridging the Generation Gap

In-Between
Bridging the Generation Gap

Devender Singh

BLACK EAGLE BOOKS
Dublin, USA | Bhubaneswar, India

Black Eagle Books
USA address:
7464 Wisdom Lane
Dublin, OH 43016

India address:
E/312, Trident Galaxy, Kalinga Nagar,
Bhubaneswar-751003, Odisha, India

E-mail: info@blackeaglebooks.org
Website: www.blackeaglebooks.org

First International Edition Published by
Black Eagle Books, 2024

IN-BETWEEN
(Bridging the Generation Gap)
by **Devender Singh**

Copyright © Devender Singh

All rights reserved. No part of this publication may be reproduced, stored in a retrieval system, or transmitted, in any form or by any means, electronic, mechanical, photocopying, recording or otherwise without the prior permission of the publisher.

Cover & Interior Design: Ezy's Publication

ISBN- 978-1-64560-535-5 (Paperback)
Library of Congress Control Number: 2024934957

Printed in the United States of America

Preface

Drama is an inimitable class of literature, and it is more so in case of Indian writing in English, being one of the hitherto much discounted genres. Performing arts focus on the representation of life and human experience through dialogue, action and performance. The play *In-Between* by Devender Singh, a playwright par excellence, does accomplish all the decrees of admirable drama. The Plot, Characters, Setting, Conflict, Theme, Dialogue, Stage Directions and the Characteristics of the Play are coherently maintained here. The Acts and Scenes, the Script, Characters and Casting, Stage Design and the Dramatist's Vision make *In-Between* highly readable and decipherable.

Devender Singh addresses the existential dilemma of human life in the play *In-Between* in a philosophical and psychological custom that explores the inherent challenges, uncertainties of his characters who are absolutely, cheerfully flesh-and-blood, here-and-now. He questions the individuals' lives that grapple with their existence. Existentialism, a philosophical movement that emerged in the 19th and 20th centuries, probes into these profound questions, and this play fits into the designs of Existentialism. Singh talks about the meaning and purpose of the lives of his characters while attributing freedom, flexibility, inclusivity and responsibility to them. The characters translate Singh's philosophy that with freedom comes the burden of responsibility. The existentialist dilemma in the play involves navigating the tension between the freedom to make choices and the responsibility for the consequences of those choices. Existentialism emphasizes the importance of authenticity and individuality. The dilemma arises when individuals must confront societal expectations, conformism and the challenge of staying true to themselves. Existentialists explore the tension between the desire for authentic connections with others and the inherent isolation that comes with being an individual. How can one find meaningful connections in a seemingly indifferent or absurd world? Singh attempts to address this question in the play. His empirical dilemma involves confronting anxiety and uncertainty about the future, the nature of reality and the limits of human knowledge. How does the awareness of one's finite existence influence the choices and actions made during a lifetime? The characters in *In-Between* grapple with the concept of the absurd—the idea that life lacks inherent meaning, and individuals must confront this lack of meaning in their pursuit of a meaningful existence. They face the challenge of constructing their identities in a world that may not provide clear guidelines or inherent purpose. The search for identity becomes a key aspect of their existential journey. Their dilemmas are not only philosophical but also psychological challenges that they experience throughout their lives. Existentialist thinkers like Jean-Paul Sartre, Albert Camus, and Søren Kierkegaard have explored these themes, offering insights into how individuals can navigate the complexities of human existence and find meaning and authenticity in their lives. Following the great masters, the existential dilemma of the play *In-Between* is an ongoing exploration that invites individuals to engage in self-reflection, introspection and the continual search for personal significance in the face of life's inherent uncertainties.

The existential dilemma of human life and the concept of balancing gender binaries -- both explore the complex aspects of human existence and identity in this play. Singh critically engages with the balancing of gender binaries and he addresses the traditional and often rigid cataloguing of gender. Contemporary considerations of gender in the play *In-Between* emphasize its fluid and spectrum-like nature. Rather than adhering strictly to binaries and categories, the characters of Singh identify outside or between the traditional male and female responsibilities and stereotypes. Balancing gender binaries involves challenging and redefining societal expectations and roles associated with masculinity and femininity. Efforts to break free from the gendered-pigeon-holes contribute to a more inclusive and diverse understanding of gender expression in the play. Recognizing the intersectionality of identity, which includes aspects such as race, ethnicity, sexuality, and socio-economic status, is crucial in understanding how individuals experience and navigate gender in the play, and Singh masters that art. Achieving a balance in gender binaries in the play In-Between involves fostering an inclusive society and accepting it where individuals are free to express their identity without the anxiety of discrimination or marginalisation.

Singh also highlights the ways in which generational divide within the traditional middle-class Indian family leaves a deep chasm in human relationships and personal identity. He doesn't attempt to offer moral solutions to this dilemma but instead makes it interact with the other themes elegantly. The inevitability of conflict and the fragility of identity make up the dramatic core of the play and allow the characters to embark on a journey of self-realization and growth. Singh's colloquial touch helps the readers connect with these characters intimately and empathize with their predicaments. One is forced to ponder over the ways in which a disturbed family sends ripple effects that impact the overall psyche of a society.

In fact, the existential dilemma of human life involves the profound questions surrounding existence, freedom and meaning, while balancing the easy binaries. Singh focuses on challenging and redefining traditional notions of identity and mien of his characters. He summons reflections on the complexities of human self and the enduring quest for validity and equality.

The novelty and the creativity of Singh lie in his experimentation with genre and technique. For him, truly, 'technique is discovery'.

Professor Nandini Sahu
Creative Writer & Folklorist
www.kavinandini.blogspot.in
www.nandinisahu.in

From the Playwright's Pen

'In-Between' is a story that unveils the inherent truth within every human being across different eras, a truth suppressed in the mental fabric of civilized societies. While individuals in any epoch may be considered modern within their temporal context, it is only the passage of time that categorizes them as traditionalists, conservatives, or unconventional. Drawing from the Indian knowledge tradition, the play aligns with the concept that, after completing the initial two stages of life, individuals enter an intermediate phase where they cannot revert to the past nor fully embrace the future. In contemporary times, this juncture typically manifests after the age of 40 or somewhere between the ages of 40 and 50.

During this phase, a person finds himself in a unique situation – neither entirely old nor entirely young. Despite having youthful enthusiasm, arrogance, mischief, and numerous strenuous efforts, time comes in the way of life with many punctuation marks. While responsibilities take root in the mind, with its baggage, maturity begins to desire the transformation of baked, half-baked and unbaked emotions through the crucible of experience. It's a peculiar juncture where children evolve into young individuals, driven by their emerging interests, while middle-aged individuals find their interests deeply embedded in their minds, exerting control over their lives. This marks the transitional period, perhaps a phase that renders a person vulnerable even when physical strength persists.

Individuals with jobs encounter heightened challenges. As one navigates through the complexities of life, a multitude of experiences surfaces, leading to an overwhelming workload that extends from the office into the home, blurring boundaries. This brings individuals to a crossroads where they neither fully embrace a domestic lifestyle nor remain solely dedicated to their professional roles. In this scenario, equilibrium becomes disrupted, sparking conflicts between spouses. Coping with such challenges demands a unique skill set that may not be possessed by everyone. Natural skill to deal with such situations are not found in everyone as nature distributes its gifts unevenly, and relying on fate for mercy is ultimately futile.

Women face more profound challenges compared to men. Given the revered role of mothers across cultures, their focus tends to lean towards their children rather than their husbands. The existence of a generation gap among spouses and children leads to divergent ideologies. Within this dynamic, a woman, referred to as a mother, finds herself navigating conflicting loyalties. Struggling to decide between her children and husband, her heart remains with the former while her mind remains with the latter. Remarkably, she manages to maintain a more delicate balance than men. Despite a deeper affection for her children, she retains her commitment to her husband. Men can learn valuable lessons in this balancing act from women.

This play delves into a crucial theme cantered around human values that get trampled between the destructive forces of false pride and ego. The negative influences of position-related arrogance, male-centric pride, and unchecked greed can degrade an individual to the point where they lose awareness of their responsibilities and disregard the rights of others. By the time the completely ruined individual realises and acknowledges the unfairness of their actions, the clock signals the end of their time.

Throughout the world, people in various cultures have developed numerous arts to simplify and enhance human life. However, with time, disinterest or materialism often obscures these cultural advancements. This pattern is indicative of a natural phenomenon. As civilizations and cultures peak, their decline becomes inevitable. Yet, within every downfall lies opportunities that illuminate new paths for life. Despite the portrayal of numerous challenges, this play also highlights solutions rooted in the Indian knowledge tradition. It is expected that this work effectively conveys the significance of the pure Indian philosophy encapsulated in *Sarve Bhavantu Sukhinah* and resonates with discerning readers.

Dr. Devender Singh
Department of English
University of Delhi , New Delhi-110007

List of Characters

Ramesh	:	A man in his late 40s who serves as a deputy secretary in Central Secretariat
Jeevan	:	Friend of Ramesh who also serves as a deputy secretary in Central Secretariat
Manju	:	Wife of Ramesh
Jyoti	:	Wife of Jeevan
Vinay	:	Son of Ramesh and Manju
Sangeeta	:	Colleague and beloved of Vinay
Kunal	:	Son of Jeevan and Jyoti
Anju	:	Wife of Kunal
Sahiram	:	Father of Sangeeta who is an arrogant police officer
Badami	:	Mother of Sangeeta who is very emotional and spiritual
Angoori	:	Sister of Badami; the victim of her own fate
Badlu	:	Brother of Sahiram; a selfish person
Sunita	:	Wife of Badlu; a wicked woman
Sonu	:	The Gigolo who tries to rape Sangeeta
Avtar Singh	:	A friend of Sahiram, an honest police officer and a saviour of Sangeeta

Hakim Amma : An old villager possessing knowledge of Ayurveda

Doctor : One who treats Badami

Nurse : An employee in the hospital where Badami is being treated

Sadashiv Nath : A Sage and a spiritual Guru in Haridwar

Act-I Scene-I

Time-1:30 PM

Location- A Park near Ramesh and Jeevan's office in the heart of Delhi.

Ramesh and Jeevan work in the same office and have come to the nearby park during lunch break.

Jeevan	:	Today you have already come and sat down. Do you masticate your food or swallow it directly. It seems my friend has trapped a fish.
Ramesh	:	Wicked! Everything looks yellow to the jaundiced eyes. You see everyone as you are. Go and take your dose. I mean smoke otherwise, here only, you will collapse talking to me.
Jeevan	:	Do you come here every day seemingly after consuming acid? Your facial expressions consistently reflect your irritation. Nonetheless, an indisputable truth remains: regardless of any anger you may harbour, in your half-sleeved shirt and matching pants, you maintain a youthful appearance. So, if I make a few comments, what is harm in it? And yes, I know everything very well; your

	personal assistant visits you frequently, whether there is a specific purpose or not.
Ramesh	: Jealousy clings to those who possess it. Shrewd, mine revolves around me, but you persistently chase yours. You; the unfortunate one, orbit like a satellite but lack the courage to approach her, even by an inch. You continue to yearn.
Jeevan	: So what? We're still young and free to roam around. I don't know whether I am a satellite or not, but you are definitely a celestial body in my horoscope, that too a dirty one, Saturn Rahu Ketu type. Don't pretend to be overly virtuous. Since the new PA arrived, you come every day with extra makeup, dyed hair, and fragrance. The poor guy has no other choice, right? Well, mind is after all mind; fickler than mercury, isn't it? It has nothing to do with age. By the way, let me share something, we are not good people either.
Ramesh	: You must be a lousy person. Scoundrel, I maintain discipline. What have you just said, Shani, Rahu-Ketu type? O utter fool! Just know this, someone with strong Shani, Rahu-Ketu in horoscope becomes a king; the emperor.
Jeevan	: What do you mean by that? Are you the stronger one?
Ramesh	: Absolutely right, I'm the stronger one that's why you are the king of your

	department. A powerful friend makes even a dunce a king.
Jeevan	: You're right, brother. In reality, I'm a dunce that has spent decades carrying your burden.
Ramesh	: Hey fool, shut your mouth and let's head to the office. Lunch break is about to end.
Jeevan	: Of course, brother. My time is up now, and the PA's time starts.
Ramesh	: Jealousy, oh, your jealousy. One day, it will definitely turn your heart into coal.
Jeevan	: A friend's heart is always considered smaller than a P.A.'s. Jealously is natural. I am helpless. Despite having fierce fire within, I'm not completely burnt. You must have heard this couplet of Kabir.

Lakadi jal koila bhai, koila jal bhai raakh,
Main bawari aisi jalii, koila bhai naraakh.

(Having burnt, the wood turned into coal and the coal into ash I, the fool also burnt but not to coal or ash)

Ramesh	: I've mentioned before that a pair of jaundiced eyes always have yellow hue. Let's refrain from discussing philosophy during our work hours. What I mean is, our break time has come to an end, and it's time to get back to earning for the sake of our children.
Jeevan	: Oh, yes, I forgot about the children. How's Vinay doing?

Ramesh	:	Brother, Vinay is a gem. Honestly speaking, Vinay is my strength as well as weakness. He's due for a promotion. After that, we'll arrange his marriage.
Jeevan	:	That's wonderful. Our children are our primary motivation. Through all the positive and negative actions, sins and virtues, we've dedicated a lot of effort to our jobs. Their achievements also serve as a source of inspiration for us.
Ramesh	:	Alright, tell me, how's Kunal doing? Is everything going well in his married life?
Jeevan	:	Up until now, we've been fortunate. Regarding the future, it's uncertain. Kunal and his spouse both have jobs, which is quite helpful. They may now consider the prospect of constructing a comfortable home.
Ramesh	:	Good. Rest assured; everything will be fine. (Looking at the clock) Oh! Time flies when we're engrossed in conversation. Let's get back to work now.
Jeevan	:	(In a sarcastic tone) Yes, indeed, sir. After all, it's time for *Kamdev* (the god of desires).

With that, both of them burst into laughter and head back to their offices.
The curtain falls.

******

Act-I Scene-II

Time- 1:00 pm
Location-A Park near Vinay's office in Gurugram.
Vinay (Ramesh's son) is sitting with Sangeeta in a park near his office. Both work at the same position and love each other. They often come here during lunch time.

Vinay	:	(Seeing Sangeeta lost in thoughts) Why are you sitting quiet today, Sangeeta? Why don't you say something? What happened?
Sangeeta	:	(Distracted by Vinay's call) Na ...Na... Nothing. No specific issue.
Vinay	:	What do you mean by nothing specific? There must be something that has locked your lips. Is there anything worth hiding from me? If so, I won't ask again.
Sangeeta	:	Okay, so you won't ask. Alright, tell me, have you ever heard those lines of a song?
Vinay	:	Which song and which lines? (Vinay asked with a slight smile.)
Sangeeta	:	These ones- *Sunaana bhi jinhein mushkil, chhupana bhi jinhein mushkil. Jara tu hi bata ae dil vo afsane kahaan jaaye.*

(Difficult to reveal, difficult to hide, O heart! Tell me where such stories should be kept.)

Vinay : Why are you trying to create riddles? Just tell me clearly, what's the issue?

Sangeeta : Riddles don't get solved, Vinay. An age passes away carrying them on tongue but no answer is received from anywhere. Firstly, life itself is a riddle, and even the greater one is love. Till date I have not understood what life is all about.

Vinay : You're adding riddles to riddles and mixing philosophy with it. Come on Sangeeta, tell me, what's the matter?

Sangeeta : It's nothing, Vinay. There are just a few memories of the past that neither let me live nor die.

Vinay : It's your habit to think needlessly. When your present and future are sitting right in front of you, what's the use of going back to the past?

Sangeeta : This mind is a strange creation of God, Vinay. Things we should forget keep coming back, and what we should remember disappears from the memory.

Vinay : Now finally, tell me what's bothering you.

Sangeeta : (Plucking a blade of grass from the lawn and playing with it, she says to herself) What if Vinay leaves me when he knows the truth? No, no, I don't want to lose Vinay.

Vinay : How many experiments will you

	conduct on this blade of grass? If you're not going to tell anything, let's head to the office.
Sangeeta	: Vinay, this blade of grass is lifeline for those who are drowning. That's why it's worth examining closely.
Vinay	: This straw piece is the support of the destitute. There is a strong human being sitting next to you, so why worry about it?
Sangeeta	: When my mother was perfectly fine, she used to say that time is not trustworthy, so a person must be aware of his own strength.
Vinay	: So, you don't trust my strength?
Sangeeta	: I'm well aware of your strength, but I don't trust my destiny.
Vinay	: Then write down your destiny and get out of this dilemma or allow me to write your fate for you?
Sangeeta	: This is the irony of life. The Divine examines each individual, and what's intriguing is that everyone faces unique test scenarios. No one's efforts will help in someone else's examination, and nobody can merely imitate another. Each person must independently steer and succeed in their own examination.
Vinay	: I might not possess the ultimate wisdom about life, but I am certain about this: you've misjudged life. Life encompasses emotions and the significance of heartfelt prayers. In challenging life situations,

		the heartfelt prayers from our dear ones profoundly influence our triumph.
Sangeeta	:	Yes, that would be true. But dear life teaches everyone different lessons. In my life, certain events have occurred where neither prayers nor medicines have worked.
Vinay	:	You might have delved deeper into the philosophy of life than I have, but I wonder why emotions exist if they serve no purpose. I find solace in my mother's prayers, as they are a source of impenetrable shield for me.
Sangeeta	:	What if someone doesn't have a mother?
Vinay	:	Sangeeta, you're stepping beyond the limits of respect. Remember, your mother is still with us. A mother, no matter how unwell and vulnerable, can fiercely fight for her children, even with Yamaraj (the god of death). It's only a mother whose unwavering emotions are beyond question.
Sangeeta	:	My intention is not to disrespect my mother in any way, but the one staying with me isn't my real mother.
Vinay	:	What? What are you saying? The person living with you isn't your real mother. Then who is she, and where is your real mother?
Sangeeta	:	(Turning her head slightly, says to herself) Come what may, today I must tell Vinay the truth. I can't keep him in the dark any longer.

Vinay	:	What's going through your mind? Say something, please.
Sangeeta	:	I've told you so many times that I want to share something about my past, but you're never ready to listen.
Vinay	:	Today, you've revealed a secret about your mother that has piqued my curiosity. I'm not prepared to hear anything else right now.
Sangeeta	:	But why? Did my words upset you?
Vinay	:	No, nothing's bothering me. Just check the time. We're already 15 minutes past lunchtime. We'll have to rush. The project director is having an important meeting. I'll listen to your story some other time. Let's go. We need to get to the office soon.

They both get up and walk briskly toward their office.
The Curtain falls

******

Act-I Scene-III

Time- 6 pm
Location- Ramesh's house in Uttam Nagar, Delhi.
Ramesh and Manju's son Vinay have just come from office.

Vinay : Dad, Dad, listen, have some sweets. I got a promotion today. Within just one year, the company has entrusted me with significant responsibilities. My salary will also be increased by 20-30 thousand. Now, we can buy a bigger car and a larger house.

Ramesh : Good and bad news, don't share them together. A 20-30 thousand difference in salary is fine, but buying a big car is not a sweet sentence. I spent 15-20 lakhs on your education, and that's how you got this job. Now, I'm thinking about your marriage. The big car will certainly come. Speaking of marriage, yes, I remember something, take a day off from the office tomorrow. I've invited some people to meet you.

Manju : At least for sometimes, but enjoy the happiness of your child. You always make decisions on your own. What's the point of demanding a big car from someone? My son earns well. He can buy as many cars as you wish. Just make sure that we find him a girl, or he selects one himself. I don't want wealth; I want a beautiful, virtuous, and loving daughter-in- law.

Vinay, after hearing his parents' conversation, leaves the room.

Ramesh : Are you so beautiful and virtuous that you'll find such a daughter-in-law? Who's giving you wealth and riches? In fact, you're not his mother; but his enemy. Don't even think of discussing this in his presence. Who is he to select a daughter-in-law? I'll choose, and she'll enter our house in a big car.

Manju : Your mind seems to be messed up. Even in this modern era, you talk about dowry. Haven't you seen how smart kids are these days? My Vinay doesn't even make eye contact with you. He should have so much freedom that he can choose his life partner on his own.

Ramesh : Stop your *Rag Bhairavi* (Unpleasant talks). Your father didn't give us anything, now, don't interfere in my son's wedding. I'll arrange the wedding the way I want.

Manju : How far will you curse my parents? Even in those days, they went far beyond their status to get me married.

Ramesh : Status, hahaha! I know everything, but who asked them to go beyond their status? They could find a boy equal to

		their status. Why did they marry their girl to a government servant? Your father is really a clever hunter.
Manju	:	No matter how much dowry the girl's side gives, even if they give everything they have, the groom's side is never satisfied.
Ramesh	:	Girl side? With what misconception are you living? You were never a girl. You were born a full-grown woman, that too at the ripe age of 30-35. To sell such a cheap product, one has to pay a lot.
Manju	:	It's a good thing I came matured, this house is settled. If some budding immature had come, by now, either you'd have devoured her uncooked or she would have withered away on her own.
Ramesh	:	These days, your tongue seems to be working overtime. While stuck up at a railway crossing, a jennet thinks that the train won't pass until she leaves the track.
Manju	:	I've endured enough and won't tolerate more. From verbal abuse to physical violence, I've seen it all. I won't let my child bear the same.
Ramesh	:	Empty vessel sounds much. A baseless individual always engages in an argument.
Manju	:	When the guardians are no more, the dependents continue to mourn. I am helpless as my parents have passed

	away. They couldn't foresee they were handing over their daughter to a butcher. I wouldn't be experiencing these difficult times if I had any form of support.
Ramesh	: Support! O my dear, you have so much talent that you can create support in both your hands. You may not know that endless people revolve around you just waiting for your signal.
Manju	: Impressive! What a remarkable comment it is! I was pondering over this for quite some time – why didn't you bring in this issue earlier? When a lion is helpless, it commits suicide, but when a man is high and dry, he points a finger at a woman's character. What a disgrace it is! A man may spend the entire day away, but when he returns home, he starts tarnishing his own woman's character with baseless accusations.
Ramesh	: Stop your nonsense, or I have other ways to hold your tongue.
Manju	: I also had ways, but unfortunately, I never tried them. I do have a lot of work to do. I'm not roaming Idle to listen to your nonsense.

Saying this, Manju leaves and Ramesh starts oscillating in the courtyard of the house with his eyes red in anger and fists tightly clenched.
The curtain falls.

******

Act-I Scene-IV

Time- 7:00 am
Location – Ramesh's house.
The next morning everyone got up at their own time. Ramesh did not have to go to office but got up on time. Vinay is confused whether to go to office or not. In this confusion, he comes to his mother.

Vinay	:	Mom, I need to leave for the office a bit early today. There's a lot of work, and after the promotion, I have to take on a few new responsibilities.
Manju	:	Son, today you shouldn't go to the office. Haven't you heard that your Hitler father has called a party for you? They are coming to see you.
Vinay	:	Party? What party, Mom? Am I some merchandise to be showcased and sold?
Manju	:	But, my son, you'll have to get married eventually.
Vinay	:	Mom, marriage is a major decision in one's life. I will make this choice entirely of my own accord.
Manju	:	I'll never stop you, son. Of course, marriage is a big decision, but it's essential to consider the opinions of others. Have you chosen any girl?

Vinay	:	Yes, Mom, I've selected a girl. She's the project manager in my office. We both got promoted at the same time.
Manju	:	Great! That's wonderful! If she works in your office, it's even better. When are we meeting her and her parents?
Vinay	:	I also want you all to meet her but she doesn't have a father, and her mother has been a bit mentally disturbed since her father passed away. So, we need to talk directly to her only.

Ramesh overhears the conversation and enters angrily.

Ramesh	:	Wow, my son, wow! Even ants have got wings. But remember, their wings exist for a short time and lead them to die in agony after a short flight. Listen, I am not running an orphanage where anyone can bring anyone. No one can enter my house without my permission. (Turning to Manju) And yes, you, his supporter, tell this *Ranjha* (The protagonist in great Indian love story of *Heer-Ranjha*) that he shall not go anywhere today.

Saying this, Ramesh leaves, but Vinay is unsure of how to proceed. He has never argued with his father. He wonders how to confront his father now.

Vinay	:	Mom, what is all this?
Manju	:	Howsoever tall and old it may grow, you can't have mangoes from a Neem tree, my son. Even if you irrigate it with milk, it won't bear mangoes. With age, false pride, ego, and many other biases grow bigger.

Vinay	:	But Mom, Papa should also try to understand others' emotions. Others' feelings should be valued too.
Manju	:	I used to think the same way earlier, my son. I also used to believe that after the next generation becomes wise, the previous generation gives up its stubbornness, ego and prejudices but, something contrary to it happens. These people don't understand what legacy of aberration they are leaving behind for their future generations.
Vinay	:	But Mom, I can't ruin my life for someone else's false pride. I'm not a commodity; I'm a human filled with emotions. I can't just blindly accept all their baseless claims. Come what may, I need to go to the office.
Manju	:	I have seen worse days than this, my son. Many times, there are situations where you have to save one, either home or familial relationship. In such cases, our Indian tradition says, if relationships survive, more houses can be created. No one could have thought that to save relationships, even the legend like *Bhishma Pitamah* would propose the division of *Hastinapur*. But that happened.
Vinay	:	But Mom, I have to go to office today at any cost and I am leaving.

With this, Vinay leaves.
The curtain falls.

******

Act I Scene V

Time- 01:30 pm
Location – A park near Vinay's office in Gurugram.
During lunch time, Vinay and Sangeeta are sitting in a park near their office. Vinay is very upset about what happened at home this morning.

Sangeeta	:	Why are you so upset today? Did the boss pester you?
Vinay	:	No, yaar, the boss is quite pleased with me, but the super boss, I mean dad, is very angry. Dad is really upset.
Sangeeta	:	(Understanding the situation) Was there a discussion about our marriage?
Vinay	:	Yes, but how do you know about all this?
Sangeeta	:	Never mind how I came to know about it. Just tell me the whole story of what happened at home.
Vinay	:	But, today, you were going to tell me your story. How did you guess my situation?
Sangeeta	:	Life's experiences are the biggest school for a person. Based on what time has taught, I can, at least, estimate this much.
Vinay	:	Being a project manager, you can anticipate the problems that may arise

	in starting and completing a project.
Sangeeta :	Well said, sir! Now tell me, whether or not your family members are ready to get you married?
Vinay :	Yes ready, but they want me to marry a girl of their choice. They have invited the girl's family to see me today. Dad was telling Mom that the girl's family is very rich, they will give a big car, all other items and a significant amount of cash too. I was asked to stay back home, but I disobeyed and came to office. I'm scared. You can't simply estimate what may happen today!
Sangeeta :	Oh my God! It's a blunder you have committed. If your dad doesn't agree, then marry as per his wishes.
Vinay :	No, I can't deceive you. I can't allow anyone sell me in the open market.
Sangeeta :	Your parents have raised you and made you what you are. They also have some desires and right. Having accepted certain happenings as the desire of fate, we should move forward.
Vinay :	You and I also have rights. Are we born just to die struggling and suffering?
Sangeeta :	Forget about me; I hardly know my rights. Ever since my father's passing, I've been solely acquainted with my responsibilities. Sometimes, certain mishaps in life take away all human rights and turn a person into a mere workhorse, tirelessly pulling a wagon

		of duties, taking everyone to their destinations, and yet, the wagon has to return to its starting point.
Vinay	:	So, should I play along and become a character in your fate's cruel game?
Sangeeta	:	At what point of time has *Heer* been destined to meet her *Ranjha*? It's better to spend life as friends than bearing pain throughout life.
Vinay	:	Don't let the characters from stories enter real life, Sangeeta. It's better if stories remain just stories.
Sangeeta	:	Stories aren't mere happenstance; they are crafted, and characters are akin to puppets, at times swaying to the will of the Almighty, and at the others, to societal influences.
Vinay	:	But I can't accept being tied to the strings of somebody else's stubborn will, excessive ambition and ego and dance a puppet. These are not the strings that animate lifeless puppets, rather, these strangle a perfectly alive person and make him dance to their tune.
Sangeeta	:	But apart from this, we are left with no other option.
Vinay	:	I've never seen you so weak before.
Sangeeta	:	When the storm of troubles arrives, it's not strength but wisdom that's needed. Sometimes, accepting certain things is better than fighting them.
Vinay	:	Sorry, I don't agree. I understand what right and wrong are to me. I can't allow

	anyone to dictate my decisions, even if he happens to be my father.
Sangeeta	: But I don't want to be the reason of conflict in your family.
Vinay	: Who wants a conflict? Conflicts have nor arisen because of you, Sangeeta. They're the result of someone's false pride and stubbornness. Come what may, I won't allow anyone to play with my life. I've given my word to you, haven't I?
Sangeet	: The tree of ambition bears the fruit of arrogance, and those who consume it are destined to end up in tears. See, Vinay, try to understand this. Stubbornness doesn't allow harmony in households; it shatters them. As far as promises are concerned, it was just a commitment to me, not to a divine entity. Earthly promises are made to the mortal beings, and shattered here on the Earth only.
Vinay	: You still don't understand me. My promise was not to you but to my own soul. Please don't teach me about slaying my own soul. And yes, homes don't get ruined by stubbornness but by ego. Stubbornness is determination that helps in achieving one's goal.
Sangeeta	: Learn to distinguish between determination and stubbornness. While even the most stubborn lapwing couldn't have dried up the ocean, it was its determination that achieved it. Stubbornness is only beneficial

	during childhood when the mind isn't spoiled by craftiness. Beyond that, it's determination that truly gets things done.
Vinay	: Your philosophical statements and strange arguments are beyond my understanding. Just tell me directly, will you marry me or not?
Sangeeta	: (Peeping into Vinay's eyes for a moment) My salary is equal to yours. Our positions are the same. I have enough money on my own. Together, we can create happiness. But life also teaches us that happiness is useless without our loved ones.
Vinay	: Talk about possibilities, not principles, Sangeeta. Theories keep changing and evolving. Tell me clearly whether you will marry me. Will you leave me a victim of someone's greed?
Sangeeta	: Then go ahead and tell your father about the property and money I possess.
Vinay	: Never! I know that as soon as he hears about your property and bank balance, he will shower you with praises. You'll become the world's most cultured and beautiful girl. But I haven't killed my conscience yet. I've loved you even before I knew nothing about your parental property.
Sangeeta	: When a gun is sufficient, why to use a cannon?
Vinay	: I don't understand at all what you say.

Just tell me whether you're willing to marry me or not.

Sangeeta : (Having noticed Vinay's stubbornness and innocence, she looks into his eyes for a moment) I know that our marriage will bring storms into your life. But so far, I've passed my life navigating storms in the world's oceans. If you're the sailor, once again I am ready to brave the storm, I have full faith in you, Vinay. But remember, even skillful navigators, after rescuing the boat from many storms, often end up in a place where nothing from their old world can be found.

Vinay : You're worried that you might encounter trouble because of me, aren't you?

Sangeeta : I've already transcended the limits of fear. Now, I roam around having courage to face the consequences. Still, at any cost, I don't want to go against your parents.

Vinay : I've also never contradicted my parents. From school time onwards, I've never been in the wrong crowd of friends. I always considered my mom, dad, and sister as my friends and kept enjoying their company. Since childhood, certain values have been instilled in me. Not only against my parents, but I also never dared to use harsh words against anyone older than me.

Sangeeta : This decency and etiquette of yours are

		my weaknesses. A woman who receives true love and respect from her husband conquers the whole world. You possess both these virtues.
Vinay	:	My mother instilled in my character the courage to hold on to the truth even in the most adverse circumstances. Perhaps that's why my courage and values, today, stand firmly opposite to each other.
Sangeeta	:	The paths you've chosen are fraught with difficulties, and they might lead you to solitude in the wilderness. You should have thought about this choice many times before making it.
Vinay	:	Overthinking either delays decisions or prevents them from being taken. I am confident that truth will protect my values and lead me to the right destination. In case that destination is *Khandavaprastha*, we will turn it into *Indraprastha* with our determination and hard work.
Sangeeta	:	So, you've sounded the bugle of rebel against societal norms.
Vinay	:	It's not a rebel, Sangeeta; it's the beginning of change. If changing values that no longer serve humanity and society is considered as rebel, then yes, it's a rebel.
Sangeeta	:	I'm a bit scared. It's the first time in my life that I've seen truth and values come face to face.

Vinay	:	If you trust me, don't get afraid. Such extraordinary situations require the upholding of values. If I leave it unfinished, someone else will complete. Nature doesn't rely on a single individual only. Trust me, keep supporting me. No matter how difficult the circumstances are, I will emerge victorious.
Sangeeta	:	I will always be with you, but you must listen to and understand some things from me first.
Vinay	:	Alright, I'll listen. If someone else had posed conditions on my love, I might have refused, but I'm ready to hear your story.
Sangeeta	:	(Looking into Vinay's eyes) I don't want to lose you, Vinay.
Vinay	:	Then give me all the rights that make it easier for me to have you.

Sangeeta takes Vinay's hand in hers, closes her eyes, and silently surrenders herself.
The curtain falls.

******

Act-II Scene-I

Time - 2:00 PM
Location - Sangeeta's house in the small village of Rainagiri in the foothills of the Aravalli range in Alwar district of Rajasthan.

This story hails from the time when Vinay had recently commenced his employment at a multinational company following the completion of his engineering degree. Eager to hear Sangeeta's tale, he conveyed to his mother that he would be away on a work-related trip for approximately three to four days, thus unable to return home during that period. Simultaneously, Sangeeta had informed her maid that she will arrive home later than usual, approximately two to three hours behind schedule. Sangeeta confides in Vinay that she is uncertain when her own story had its inception, but she can pinpoint the moment she grasped its significance and her role within it. She delves into her school days, specifically when she was in the 9th grade, recounting how her father frequently subjected her mother to physical abuse. On one fateful day, upon returning home from school, she discovered that her father had already assaulted her mother. Her arrival was met with her father's immediate eruption of anger.

Sahiram (Sangeeta's father): Look! Here comes the inauspicious, ill-fated girl. Now, tell her your moan story. Shed those crocodile tears.

Badami : (Wiping her tears with the end of her sari) Beware of calling my daughter ill-

	fated. Don't forget that all the blessings in your life occurred after her birth.
Sahiram	: You uncivilized woman! It seems that you haven't been fully treated yet. Your tongue is as sharp as scissors. I'll teach you a lesson now, wait a moment. (With this, Sahiram begins to beat Badami with a wood stick.) Don't you know, Sahiram is never wrong, and you, a wretch, are trying to prove me wrong?
Sangeeta	: (Running to her mother and clutching her father's legs) Papa, please don't assault Mom.
Sahiram	: (Holding Sangeeta by her ponytail and shoving her onto a nearby chair) You unruly child, you don't know that children shouldn't argue with their father. You're a bastard. Who knows whose child you are? I am Sahiram. You should also know that Sahiram is never wrong.
Sangeeta	: (With tears in her eyes) Please, don't say that, Papa. There's nothing wrong with Mom. She works all day, manages the household by sewing clothes. Even uncle and aunt keep fighting with Mom all the time.
Sahiram	(With a sinister smile) : Impressive! Bravo. This young one, born to this bitch, is attempting to challenge me. It's a well-known fact that individuals with negative intentions often attract unsavoury allies. Despite the lack

	of formal education, you've become a skilled advocate to defend this abominable woman.
Sangeeta	: Papa, please, don't say that. Mom has been tirelessly managing this home day and night. You're on duty and come home only once in a month or two. I witness her hard work every day.
Sahiram	: Shameless one! Your tongue, with its sharpness, is the most substantial proof of you being a bastard. My blood can never go against me. (Drunk Sahiram, slapped Sangeeta hard and shouted grabbing her ponytail.) Didn't you hear me? Sahiram is never wrong. Don't dare to argue with me again.
Badami	: (Seeing her daughter being beaten and losing her control, she stands up, grabs Sahiram by the collar from behind, and forcefully pulls him away to save her daughter.) Beware! I won't tolerate anyone harming my daughter.
Sahiram	: (Controlling himself and seething with anger, he picks up the same stick and violently attacks Badami.) The bitch is defying a lion. How dare you catch a police officer by the collar?
Badami	: (Feeling helpless, she clasps her hands together and pleads with Sahiram) Sannu's (Sangeeta's nick name) father, please don't hit me. I'm already very unfortunate. Oh God! I don't have a mother, father, brother, or any support,

		where should I go if I want to go?
Sahiram	:	Who said you have no one to support you? On your signal, hundreds of your supporters from this village alone will come to help you. Rather, I'm afraid you might provoke them for my murder.
Badami	:	(Crying with folded hands) Please don't say that. Apart from this girl, I have no one in this world. Show some mercy, please.
Sahiram	:	You're right, wretch. This rude girl is entirely yours. There isn't a drop of my blood in her. In my family, there was no trend to give birth to daughters. I have no sisters nor did my two brothers ever have daughters. So, where have you brought this child from? She has been so inauspicious that after her birth, no other child was ever born in this house.
Badami	:	(Facing upwards with folded hands) Oh God! How much punishment must I endure? You know my only fault is that I have faithfully upheld my role as a wife.
Sahiram	:	I don't like God's name coming from the filthy tongue of a woman like you. Stop your nonsense. I'm going to tubewell to take a shower. I'll be back soon, so my bag should be packed, and the food should be ready by then. I have to reach my duty on time.

Irritated, Sahiram leaves in anger.

Sangeeta	:	(Crying) When will all of this end,

	Mom? We're tired of these undeserved punishments every day. It's better if he kills us.
Badami	: (Suffering and crying) Evil doesn't end so quickly, my dear. First, it causes a heavy loss to goodness.
Sangeeta	: (Crying while comforting her mother and gently massaging her mother's injured hand) But this is even more savage than animals. Look, it has started swelling, and it seems your hand is fractured. There are bruises all over your body. Still, you're trying to pack his bag and prepare food. Mom, I can't bear to see you in this condition.

A little later, Sahiram returns, and leaves without being merciful to Badami's condition. Sahiram's posting was at the Suratgarh police station, which takes nearly 10 hours to reach from his village. He comes for a day or two once in a month or two, but he repeats this drama every time before he leaves. After Sahiram leaves, Sangeeta suggests her mother go to the doctor for her treatment.

| Sangeeta | : I've never seen such a heartless person so far. You've got a fracture in your hand, and he didn't even bother to have a look at it. Don't delay any further; Mom, let's go to the doctor before your injury worsens. |
| Badami | : Where will the money come from? Your father may not be a good person, but he doesn't accept bribes. Once he made a promise to his father that he wouldn't |

	bring home a single illicit penny. Whatever we have, we need to manage within this meagre salary. When your grandfather passed away, he had also assigned your uncle's portion of the debt to your father. If we count from today, it will require an additional three to four years to settle *Bohra's* (The Rich money lender) outstanding debt.
Sangeeta	: But, Mom, why would a good person needlessly assault his wife and children? Children usually learn from their parents. What can I learn from my father? Drinking, troubling the family, baseless suspicions, and unwarranted violence or abusive language. I just can't understand what our fault is!
Badami	: Don't think like that, Sannu Beta. Do you know *Prahlad* suffered so much at the hands of *Hiranyakashyap*, yet he never lost faith? After all, God's justice has its own way.
Sangeeta	: Mom, you're truly great. Even after this horrible episode, you talk about God's justice. Why trouble God in every matter? We should handle certain issues ourselves. Now, tell me when are we visiting the doctor?
Badami	: What is the benefit of visiting a doctor, dear? In the next neighbourhood, there's an elderly Hakim (herbalist) Amma. I've heard that she can mend broken bones. Let's go to her. But wait

	a bit, my legs are paining a lot, I can't walk right now.
Sangeeta	: If you can't go, then I'll call Hakim Amma here. Let me go and bring her right now.

Sangeeta runs towards Hakim Amma's house and returns with her a short while later. Entry of Hakim Amma.

Hakim Amma	: What deeds of past life have got you a butcher husband? He's beaten you like an animal. The bone in your hand is broken. It will take some time to heal.
Badami	: What should we do, Mother? We'll have to endure what's destined. Please treat my hand quickly.
Hakim Amma	: I've never seen a cow-woman (innocent) like you. (Turning towards Sangeeta) Quickly grind some millet, add turmeric and mustard oil to it. And yes, I'll prepare bamboo splints. Give me some oil too. I'll massage your mother's hand.
Sangeeta	: Yes, Amma. (Handing over the oil and bamboo stick to Hakim Amma) Here you go, Amma. Now, I'll start cooking the millet.

In a short while, Sangeeta cooks the millet on the hearth.

Hakim Amma	: I've applied the paste to your mother's hand and tied the splints with bandages. I'll leave now. I'll come again tomorrow.

Hakim Amma Exits

Sangeeta	: Mom, your hand is swollen. It's already evening and going to be dark soon. How long will you endure the pain? I'll get you a painkiller from the doctor.

Badami : No, my dear, please stay here for the time being. Besides you, there is no one else I can turn to. The emotional pain I'm going through is even more excruciating than the physical pain in my hand, and it's eating me away from within. Hakim Amma has provided some pieces of Vijaysar wood (A pain killer herb), along with a few other herbs known for their pain-relief properties. Please prepare a mixture by boiling them in milk. I will have it. It should help alleviate my pain.

While Badami applies oil to her legs and body and converses, it's 3 AM. The slight relief from the pain helps Badami fall asleep. A while later, they both fall asleep. Hakim Amma continues to visit every day for a week, changing the bandages.

A week later in the Morning, Entry of Hakim Amma.

Hakim Amma : A week has passed, but no improvement is seen in your mother's health. Moreover, her condition has worsened to the extent that she is completely bed-ridden. Call your father and ask him to come home quickly. I am quite concerned about her worsening conditions. Go and phone your father. Tell him that your mother's health is falling.

Exits Hakim Amma

Entry of Hakim Amma, followed by Sahiram.

Sahiram : (Having entered his home says with irritation) Why are you lying there pretending to be ill? Will you let me work, or not? It's not like an irregular

		job where I can come and go whenever I want. In the police department, getting leave is very difficult.
Hakim Amma	:	(Adjusting Badami's bandage) Hey Sahiya! Why are you yelling at her? It seems you have lost your mental balance. I have never seen a woman as patient as your wife. She's been enduring irregular menstruation for three years, and you have been blind to it.
Sahiram	:	What happened, Hakim Amma? Why are you purging this drama queen's irritation at me?
Hakim Amma	:	Look, son, you're the police personnel, and you might even have the power to lock me up, still I'll speak the truth. I've also seen the world and played with my fourth generation in my lap. But I've never seen a heartless butcher like you. You've beaten her so badly that her bones are broken and joints are dislocated. If she were as cruel as you, she would have broken your face in return.
Sahiram	:	Amma, you seem to be out of your senses today. Did you have some *Tharra* (local liquor)?
Hakim Amma	:	If I had consumed it, your face wouldn't be intact now. Listen carefully, I can mend broken bones of her hand, but I cannot treat the irregular uterus discharge issues. It's beyond my

	capacity. Her pulse tells me that if we don't treat it soon, her life is a matter of a few days.
Sahiram	: Nothing will happen to her, Amma. But if you insist, I'll take her to the city tomorrow and have her checked.

Hakim Amma exits.
The curtain falls.

******

Act-II, Scene-II

Time : 11:00 AM
Location : Matsya Hospital in Alwar district, Rajasthan.
After taking Badami to the city hospital, doctors immediately advised various tests and check-ups, and she was admitted to the hospital. Sahiram calls Sangeeta.

Sahiram	:	Hello, Sannu. I won't be able to come back today. The doctors have admitted your mother to the hospital. They have advised several tests, so stay at your uncle's home tonight.
Sangeeta	:	Alright, Dad. Is Mom okay? Please take care of her.
Sahiram	:	Yes, yes, she'll be fine. Nothing will happen to her. Just do as I told you. And, tell your uncle to come over. He will attend to your mother by the time I return taking a few days off.
Sangeeta	:	Alright, Dad, I'll inform Uncle.
Two days later		
Sahiram	:	(Calling Sangeeta) Hello, Sannu. Why didn't you tell your uncle that I've called him to the city?
Sangeeta	:	Hello, Dad. I did tell him, but he said he had some urgent work and he would talk to you. How is Mom now?

Sahiram	:	Okay, that's fine. I'll talk to him. Until I arrive, just stay at your uncle's home. I am waiting for the remaining test reports of your mother. I will receive them by this evening, and then I'll talk to you.
Sangeeta	:	Alright, Dad.
Sahiram	:	(To himself) Badlu neither called nor came. What could be the reason? I've been worried for the past two days. He should have at least contacted me. (Dials Badlu's contact by taking his cell phone out of his pocket) Hello, Badlu. Didn't Sannu tell you that your sister-in-law is unwell? You didn't come. I was waiting for you.
Badlu	:	I didn't know anything, and Sanu also didn't tell me. What happened to sister-in-law? Where are you right now?
Sahiram	:	I'm in the city. Your sister-in-law is admitted here. We will receive her test reports today in the evening, and then the position will be clear.
Badlu	:	Alright, brother, I have an important work to finish. Right now, I'm sitting somewhere with someone. Please take care of sister-in-law.
Sahiram	:	(After ending the call, thinking like a police officer) He doesn't seem to care that his brother and sister-in-law are in trouble. Maybe Badami was right. No worries; I'll check all the reports first and then think over this.

Badami	:	(Seeing Sahiram concerned and distressed) Don't worry. I still have the strength in me. Sannu is not the type of child who wouldn't obey you. Your brother might have forgotten. Do one thing; leave me here and go to your work. I'll manage myself until you come back.
Sahiram	:	(To himself) I'm a policeman. I can at least estimate that someone might be lying or telling the truth.

A Nurse enters

Nurse	:	(To Sahiram) Are you Badami's attendant?
Sahiram	:	Yes, I am.
Nurse	:	You have been called by the doctor. The patient's test reports have been received. The same needs to be discussed.
Sahiram	:	Alright, I am coming right now.

Sahiram enters the doctor's room

Doctor	:	Are you here with Badami?
Sahiram	:	Yes, I am. She is my wife. Doctor, if the reports have arrived, please tell us what has happened.
Doctor	:	Who all are there in your family? How many children do you have?
Sahiram	:	It's just the three of us – myself, my wife and my daughter who is in the ninth standard. She's quite young. But please tell me what has happened.
Doctor	:	Your wife has uterine cancer, and it's in the last stages.
Sahiram	:	(Shockingly) What? Cancer! How did this happen?

Doctor	:	It happened due to your negligence.
Sahiram	:	My negligence? But how, Doctor? Firstly, so much bad has happened to me and on top of that you are blaming me.
Doctor	:	Yes, it's your negligence. After going through her case history, it's clear that she has been suffering from irregular menstruation and bleeding for three to four years, but no one cared for her.
Sahiram	:	(Bowing his head) Yes, that's true. I didn't have enough time while working in the police force to give attention to my family.
Doctor	:	What kind of a person are you? You left your own wife to die. A husband should be aware of what health issues his wife is facing.
Sahiram	:	Yes Doctor Sahib, you are right. I have made a mistake. Whatever has happened, I cannot bring it back, but please tell me what to do now.
Doctor	:	(Angrily) Mistake? It's not just a mistake; you have committed a terrible crime, and it's going to be life claiming for her. Now, tell me, who else is with you here?
Sahiram	:	Right now, there's no one else, but I can call someone from my family.
Doctor	:	Then, do this quickly; call someone immediately. Your wife's case is critical. We need to do surgery as soon as possible. You also need to make arrangements for

		around 40-50 thousand rupees. We will perform her surgery tomorrow at 10 in the morning.
Sahiram	:	Alright, sir. I'll call my family from the village, and I'll deposit the money within an hour or two. There's a bank right in front of the hospital. I'll deposit money at the reception.
Doctor	:	Please do so, and pray for her. Saving her life will be challenging, but we will do our best to extend her life from six months to a few years.
Sahiram	:	(With signs of worry on his face) Thank you very much, Doctor.

Sahiram exits the doctor's room

Sahiram	:	(Dialing a number on his phone) Hello, Badlu. Can you hear me?
Badlu	:	Yes, brother. I can hear you. Your voice is coming through.
Sahiram	:	Badlu, your sister-in-law has to undergo a major surgery, so you have to come here for a day or two.
Badlu	:	(With resentment) But, brother, I have meetings scheduled for the next two days. It will be difficult for me to come. You should handle it for two days, or you can call Sunita.
Sahiram	:	(Disconnecting the call without saying anything further) During challenging moments, those who profess to be the closest often become the quickest to withdraw. Perhaps Badami had a point when she suggested that my family

members are doing nothing except deceiving me. While working in the police force, I tested the entire world, yet I couldn't assess my own family. Maybe nature prevents humans from contemplating what she doesn't want them to comprehend. Nevertheless, I refuse to surrender. I am determined to do everything on my own.

Sahiram enters Badami's room.

Badami : What happened? What did the doctor say?

Sahiram : (Hiding worry lines on his face) Nothing special. There's a tumour in your stomach. The doctors will remove it with surgery tomorrow.

Badami : But your face shows something else.

Sahiram : Why do you judge me by my appearance? The truth is what I have said.

Badami : I'm humble but not foolish. I understand everything. I've been watching your condition for three days. You haven't bathed, and you haven't even eaten properly. My intuition tells me that he won't come. You have to do everything on your own. If you consider my advice, drop me home and let me die there only.

Sahiram : I am enough on my own. I'm a police officer. I can work for two days without break.

Badami : I know. But my heart cries when I see your condition. Before you came, the

	ward boy came, placed the food plate, and left. Come, sit here, and we'll eat together.
Sahiram	: (Turning a bit emotional after hearing Badami) After so much atrocities, even a stone would start hating me. What kind of soil are you made up of, Badami?
Badami	: Don't think too much. Come and sit with me. I have only a few days of life left. Sannu's father, now let us live to the fullest.
Sahiram	: (Emotional and looking at Badami with a sense of guilt) Even after knowing that the pyramid of pain you're sitting on is created by me, you're asking me to sit near you and eat.
Badami	: (With tears in her eyes) My mother used to say that pain or happiness is the result of our own deeds. But never mind, why dwell on the past. Come, sit with me. We'll eat together.
Sahiram	: Wait for two minutes. I'll bring something from the canteen, and then we'll eat together.

Sahiram exits and returns five minutes later.

Sahiram	: (Holding a packet of food) Here, I brought some food from the canteen. Now, let's sit comfortably and eat. (Reaching into Badami's plate and offering her a piece) You eat first.
Badami	: (Silently thinking and saying to herself) It seems that with swallowing each bite, his crust of arrogance is also

	demolishing. Perhaps today, after fourteen years of exile, His Ram has returned. But sadly, I don't have much time left now.
Sahiram	: I know, but I'm still asking, what are you thinking?
Badami	: If you know, don't ask. What is happening should happen. The past troubles me. Let me enjoy these moments. (Tears rolling down from her eyes) Please, feed me more. It feels like a hunger from many lifetimes has awakened in me today.

With the fall of tears from Badami's eyes.
The curtain falls.

******

Act-II, Scene-III

Time : 11 o'clock in the morning
Location : Sahiram's home.
Badami has undergone a major surgery, and 15 days later, she is brought back home. Chemotherapy starts a month later. Sahiram's sister of distant relation has come to his home. About six months have passed since her treatment started. Sahiram is oscillating between home and his office. In the yard, there is a cot on which Badami is lying. Sangeeta is massaging her back, and Sahiram is administering medicines one by one.

Badami : How long will you stay home? Take care of your duties as well. Sannu will look after me.

Sahiram : I have requested SP Sahab to extend my leave by fifteen days. It's only after this disaster that I realized I have neither relatives nor any siblings to take care of you. Everyone just comes to show off. No one is going to help. This sister of distant relationship has come, but she spends all day sitting and backbiting in others' homes. The people who used to provoke me and create problems in our home have all disappeared.

Badami : I'm feeling a little uneasy today, Sannu's father.

Sahiram : (Trying to console Badami) Now, you're recovering. What are you worried about?

Badami : Why do you lie, Sannu's father? I don't have much time left. My mother used to tell me a story that I too had deeply engraved in my mind. Today, I want to share that story with you. Will you listen to my story?

Sahiram : Nowadays, my conscience says that I must listen to you only. Tell me, which story would you like to share?

Badami : My mother used to say that a pack of dogs, once, went to God and asked Him, "God, how much long life have you written in our destiny?" God replied, "Fifty years." Upon hearing this, the dogs said, "Have mercy on us, Lord. We can't bear 50 years wandering and getting beaten up. Please reduce it." Then, God, out of compassion, said to the dogs, "Ok, then you'll live for 14 years. And during these initial one or two years, you'll receive everyone's love, but after that, you'll face double the sufferings. Howsoever loyal you may be to anyone, you'll also face hardships, be it from humans, neighbours, relatives, or even from your own race. Both your life and death will be so painful and horrifying that there will be many sayings prevalent in the world on your death, like 'the dog bites the dog first,' 'to die a dog's death,' 'the washer man's dog is of nowhere', 'the dog can't digest *ghee*,' etc."

Sahiram : (Turning his face towards the wall and speaking gravely) For God's sake, be quiet, Sannu's mom. Now, sleep peacefully.

Badami : I'm going to be quiet only for God's sake. Going to sleep forever. You know, Sannu's Dad, that today marks our fourteenth wedding anniversary. And during these fourteen years, I've lived the life of a dog. I prayed to God every day to liberate this bitch after bearing suffering for 14 years. God heard my plea and a call for me is on the way.

Sahiram : How much more will you embarrass me, Sannu's mom? During past six months, everyone's true colors have been revealed. I wish I had understood much earlier what I do now. I myself am responsible for turning my own life into hell. What will my daughter learn from her father? I don't have any virtues left.

Badami : My intention is not to disgrace you but to share things with you that you never gave me a chance to say. Your two brothers' purpose is to exploit you. They are both characterless, which is why they have continuously made me a victim and kept humiliating me. They never liked to see this house prospering. And Baiji, the sister of your distant

	relationship, only cares about having a son. She hates my daughter. My only humble request is that after my death, take care of my Sannu. She's very innocent.
Sahiram	: (By closing the gushing eyes tightly and stopping the tears from falling.) O Omnipotent Maker, what cruel injustice is this? As I yearn to live with my beloved wife and family, and to bestow upon them all the happiness in the world, you tear our family in pieces. Have mercy, O Lord. Do not punish my daughter, Sannu, and her mother for my offences. Grant half of my remaining years to Sannu's mother, O God, so that I may live with her for a few more days, and we may perish together.

As soon as he said this, tears started flowing from Sahiram's eyes like the water of a river starts flowing with great speed as the dam breaks.

Badami	: Sannu's father, destiny has its own set of laws. Nobody is at fault in this situation. I am bearing all of the pain due to my own deeds. There has to be karma from some previous births that is currently getting in the way. Natural way of life is full of cruelty. Who knew that, putting aside all human and war values, seven legendary warriors would commit a horrific murder of their own defenseless child, Abhimanyu?

Dark clouds gathered in the sky. Badami was taken inside the room. After a short while it started raining softly outside.

Sahiram : When shall I meet such a brutal end like Abhimanyu? When will God's angels trap and destroy me?

Badami : Don't say that. Now you have to save this home. It is my karma that has been revealed. These keep following us birth after birth. One can only get rid of them after settling their accounts. But it seems that I have got the fruits of my actions also. Now it's time to calm down, Sannu's father.

Sahiram : (Looking out through the window) Oh Merciful! When will I get the fruits of my deeds? When will the provisions of the law be applied on this sinner? When will you wash away my sins? Why should I live without Badami? O Creator! This Sahiram has been proved wrong today. I confess all my sins. Let the lightening fall on me. Hey all the calamities! Pounce on me. End my life before Sannu's mother dies. More than a decade had passed since my wisdom teeth emerged. But oh God! Now, you have bestowed wisdom onto me. If you have created understanding at this juncture of life, why are you not giving me a chance to live with Badami for a few days? Please give me a chance to live with her for a few days.

Saying this, Sahiram starts crying again.

Badami : (In the midst of a heavy downpour and the rumble of thunderclouds, stretching out the edge of her shawl in Sahiram's direction) Hold this, Sannu's father. Wipe your tears away. Who knows whether or not I'll be able to offer you this shawl again after today?

Sahiram : (Wiping his tears with the shawl of Badami) Don't say that, Sannu's mother. I'll end my life without you. I want to go outside and cry in the rain because I don't want to show my tears.

Badami : Never show such cowardice. What will happen to my innocent daughter? Get her married to a good-natured boy in a respectable family.

Sahiram : Don't worry, you'll get what you want. And yes, you will be completely fine. Nothing will happen to you.

Badami : I don't know what will happen to me, but one thing you must remember is not to give my daughter to a policeman. The police and their suspicious nature have combined in such a way that they have ruined many families.

Sahiram : You are absolutely correct. Our personal lives are undoubtedly impacted by the work we do day in and day out. The police were established to uphold law and order, but after witnessing the filth of society, all of the officers have grown so distrustful that the order in their own homes has got upset.

Badami	:	That's why my father didn't want to marry me to a policeman. But what is written in our fate cannot be erased. My uncle insisted, and we got married. Anyway, leave it, what had to happen has already happened. I have something to tell you.
Sahiram	:	Say it unhesitatingly.
Badami	:	My father had only two daughters. The elder sister became a widow in her youth and troubled by her in-laws, she started living with us. Before he died, my father transferred his property in both our names. I've heard many times that your family's greedy eyes are fixed on our property. I'm afraid of any untoward happening.
Sahiram	:	Don't worry, Sannu's mother. My heart has changed at this juncture of life, so I won't seek revenge from them. However, yes, after twenty years in the police job, I've learned how to protect myself. I no longer trust these villains. I decided just yesterday that I'll bring your sister here to take care of you. I couldn't go myself, but I've asked a constable from my police station to bring her. He should be here in a little while.
Badami	:	Wow! Is Angoori really coming here? What more joyful news could there be for both of us? You've truly done a good deed.

Sahiram	:	I am thinking all along that this Sahiram hasn't done anything right so far. Well, at least you've found something that pleases you. Sannu's mother, I also have a burden on my mind. I want to say something to you.
Badami	:	If saying something lightens your heart, please do that. I'm ready to listen.
Sahiram	:	I want to apologize to you, Sannu's mother. For I've inflicted great cruelty upon you by coming under the influence of my family. These villains had erected such a wall of suspicion between us, which had biased my judgment.
Badami	:	Don't make me the victim of sins by saying that. I knew everything. I could have left you long ago if I wanted to. But I was helpless. Where could I go? I had nobody—no mother, no father, no brother, no relatives. So I endured everything happening to me, considering it my destiny. You are neither greedy nor dishonest; otherwise, you would have seized my share of the property long ago. I had deep faith that one day everything would become crystal clear to you.
Sahiram	:	What's the use of such understanding when I have nothing left in my hands? My own people have ruined me. The family is such a big deception too. They play games in the name of relationships, deceiving the feelings of someone's sensitive heart.

Badami : The important philosophy of life is that the same circumstances can't be true for everyone. For some, family is more important than self-interest, while for others, self-interest outweighs family. Family is pivotal in life. There are brothers like Bharat and Lakshman who sacrificed all their pleasures for Lord Ram. The Pandavas' life is also exemplary of best brotherhood. Even though they all had one wife Draupadi, they never doubted her character. Those who raised questions about her character faced a terrible fate.

Sahiram : How unfortunate I am! The Gem was in my heart, and my own family, by handing over the torch of suspicion, setting my home on fire, made me seek it within the labyrinth of our family connections. And when, in the midst of these complexities, a catastrophic event opened my eyes to reality, I found the corpses of my own dreams scattered here and there. (Gazing skyward) O destiny! How unjust I have been to such a wise wife!

Badami : There's no use in lamenting now, Sannu's father. Try to save my Sannu from this demon of doubt. Scriptures say that doubt weaves a complex pattern in a person's mental fabric using unseen threads of anger, jealousy, animosity, wrongdoing, and more. This creates a tangled mess in mind leading to a gradual loss of one's wisdom. Someone who lacks wisdom is undoubtedly on the path to downfall.

At around 5 in the evening, a constable from Sahiram's police station and Badami's sister enter.

Badami : (With unique mingling of tears and a sparkle in her eyes) Angoori! My sister. Come, come, and embrace me just like Lord Ram and Bharat did after fourteen years of exile.

Sahiram : (To himself) There's a different radiance on Badami's face today. It seems like there's no illness at all.

Outside, a light drizzle starts again. Badami and Angoori continue talking for about two hours.

Badami : (Turning towards Sahiram) My heart is shuddering. It feels like I am slowly heading towards unconsciousness.

Sahiram : Don't worry. We'll head to the city's big hospital even amidst the rain tonight. I'm going to arrange a vehicle right now.

Badami : With a compassionate look and unsteady voice) Please don't take me anywhere now. I don't want to go out at this hour, especially in this weather.

Sahiram : Considering your condition, I shouldn't delay.

Badami first folds her hands, then waves a hand signalling her refusal.

Sahiram : (To himself) As the night passes, Badami's condition is deteriorating.

What should I do? She's not saying anything. The rain is falling heavily. She might be sleeping. It wouldn't be right to wake her up. Let the night pass somehow, and in the early morning, I'll take her to the hospital.

Around 5 AM, Badami made an attempt to open her eyes but she could lift only half eye lids. She signalled Sahiram, Sangeeta, and Angoori to come close. She placed both of their hands in Sahiram's and gazed at him with a profound sense of compassion. In the midst of this, a sudden gust of wind entered the room through the window sprinkling a few raindrops on Badami. This was her final bath. Everyone watched in silence as her hands slipped from Sahiram's grip and hung lifeless. The thunderstorm with heavy rain reached outside their home. Perhaps the heaven started weeping loudly at the sight of the family's grief.
The curtain falls.

******

Act-II Scene-IV

Time : 6 PM
Location : A coffee shop in a shopping mall in Gurugram.

Vinay	:	How much suffering your family had to endure. But there's no point in dwelling on the past now. I've made a decision that we will get married soon, and I'll provide you with a life filled with peace and love.
Sangeeta	:	The story isn't over yet, Vinay. So, rushing to conclusions without hearing the entire story would be hasty.
Vinay	:	What? The story is still left! I've already made my decision, so what's the use of hearing the rest of it?
Sangeeta	:	I don't know about its usefulness, but without hearing the whole story, both of us can suffer.
Vinay	:	If you insist, go ahead and complete it.
Sangeeta	:	(Entering her past) Following Mom's passing away, Dad honored her final request by marrying Aunt. In just a short span of time, Aunt's health showed significant improvement. Within six months, she had assumed responsibility for both of us. Dad, too, was happy in the

	belief that he not only fulfilled Mom's last wish but also provided support to a helpless woman.
Vinay	: So, your dad had a change of heart. Better late than never. The morning starts when one wakes up.
Sangeeta	: Morning was not in our destiny so soon. It was a deception too. The night was yet to be over. We had experienced darkness so intense in life that it felt as if we were living on a planet where the day was much shorter than the Earth's and the night lasted for years. It wasn't even a year since Mom passed away when Dad's health started deteriorating. He didn't visit the doctor for many days. But when the situation got worse, he was taken to a big hospital in the city. After a complete examination, it was revealed that his sugar had reached dangerous levels, and he had got lung cancer too. The doctors informed us that his days were numbered.
Vinay	: Oh my God! Why doesn't nature let people live in peace? Is it necessary to set our happy life on fire in this way?
Sangeeta	: (As they talk, Sangeeta gets lost in her past.) One day, he was sitting on a cot in the courtyard, relaxing in the sun. He called me and Aunt over.
Sahiram	: Daughter, my days are now numbered. Before I leave to be with your mother, I want to say something to both of you.

Sangeeta	:	Please don't say such things, Dad. Nothing is going to happen to you.
Sahiram	:	Until today, Sahiram has been wrong about many things. But this is true, my daughter, my days are almost over. Now, listen carefully to what I'm saying. Your mother, your Aunt, you and I have enough property. Your uncles had their eyes fixed on this for long. They will surely try to burgle it after I'm gone. So, you need to be cautious.
Angoori	:	I won't let that happen as long as I am alive even if these people may take my life away.
Sahiram	:	What destiny are you carrying with you, Angoori? Nature didn't allow you to get happiness either from your parents or. After Badami left, I resolved to fill your life with joy, but who knew misfortune would follow you here as well?
Sangeeta	:	You're right, Dad. After Mom passed away, Aunt took care of us so well that she didn't let us feel her absence even for a moment. Does God not like our happiness?
Sahiram	:	What's God's fault in this, my child? It's the result of our own deeds. (Looking towards Angoori) Look, I've engaged a lawyer to write my will. He should be coming with it. I won't give these people a single penny. After I'm gone, you must ensure they don't plot against you and

	Sannu. The next three to four years are crucial for her.
Angoori	: I am a woman, no doubt, but not weak. I will pop out the evil eyes that gaze my Sannu.
Sahiram	: These people are very cunning. They can go to any extent. Take care of yourself and Sanu. Property has a big share in all the disputes of the world.
Sangeeta	: I will become a collector through education, Papa. No one will have the courage to look at us with wrong intentions.
Sahiram	: (Placing his hand on Sangeeta's head) Naive child! You'll achieve your dreams only when these crooks let it happen. The world is teeming with those who harbour ill intentions. Upstanding and sincere individuals often find themselves vulnerable targets. I recall your mother used to express that if people don't cause harm to each other, how will the world function? In such a scenario, everyone will achieve salvation, and there would be little left in this world to function.
Angoori	: But victory belongs to the truth. I believe these people won't be able to ruin us.
Sahiram	: That's correct. But the truth has to undergo a severe test before its victory. No one calls coal something other than coal. Only gold is put under test. Sometimes, the duration of the test can be as long as a lifetime.

Angoori	: That's why coal is destined to turn into ashes, and gold is made into jewellery and adorned.
Sahiram	: You're right. Both burn. It's just that after burning, coal turns into ashes and gold becomes pure. We must always remember that the fire that burns gold is found within coal.
Sangeeta	: What does that mean, Papa?
Sahiram	: It means that no matter how much evil bothers goodness, it shines brighter. Therefore, we should never be discouraged due to adverse circumstances.
Sangeeta	: Yes, Papa, I understand. Our troubles will eventually make us capable of success.
Sahiram	: (Looking at Sangeeta with a loving gaze) My Sannu has grown up before her time. That's good; life will become simpler. My daughter, I apologize for leaving you with the legacy of anger, enmity, jealousy, grudges, ego, and difficulties. But I'm also content that nature has taught my daughter some valuable lessons essential for her life to come. I only have a few days left. If possible, please forgive me.
Sangeeta	: (Teary-eyed, hugging her father) No, Papa. Don't say that. Adults never seek forgiveness from their children.
Sahiram	: (Patting his daughter's head) No, my child, before we lament the generation

gap, we should also consider what kind of legacy we are passing on to the generations to come. Even when Rishi Bhrigu kicked God, all he said was, "Did your foot get hurt, Maharishi?" Elder or younger, there is nothing wrong in seeking forgiveness for our mistakes.

Sangeeta : You will always be respectable to me, Dad.

Sahiram : I'm not worthy of respect. This is the right time for redemption of my sins. After meeting your mother in the heaven, if we ever get a chance to face the Divine, we will request your presence as our child once again, even if we will have to wait for it for many lifetimes. And yes, I promise you next time, I will become an exemplary husband and father.

Sangeeta : You are still a good father. Mom used to say that you never accepted a single penny as bribe. You paid for Uncle's education and marriage expenses. You are also paying the debt that was on uncle's part. In today's times, who does so much?

Sahiram : I did nothing for you. I left my innocent child in the midst of a turbulent sea. My concern is that you are currently at an age where you're neither too young nor too old. How will you deal with those dreadful snakes that stand ready around you with their fangs spread?

Sangeeta : (Coming back from her past to the

present, speaking to Vinay) Just a few days later, Papa passed away. When he was on his deathbed, he joined mine and my aunt's hands, telling her that he was entrusting Sannu to her as his legacy and leaving Aunt with me as my mother's inheritance. That's when my aunt and I became each other's support.

Vinay placed his hand on Sangeeta's shoulder and turned her face towards him. Both of Sangeeta's eyes were brimming with tears.

Vinay : What has happened had to happen. No one can defy destiny. My decision remains the same. I cannot listen to your painful story any more. Please, stop here only. Those days have already passed.

Sangeeta : (Wiping her tears with her scarf) No, Vinay, the story is not over yet, and I cannot bear to tell you an incomplete truth. Before we arrive at any conclusion, you must listen to rest of the story.

Vinay : Alright, Baba. I'll listen, but on one condition. You must give these tears a little rest now.

Sangeeta : Tears are not under my control, nor am I their boss. They flow at their own choice. All they need is suitable situations, whether in sorrow or joy. I've heard in fairy tales that in distress, even the eyes of stone images start shedding tears, a vast ocean submerges the Earth, and even the bearer of everything, the vast sky, weeps.

Vinay : Oh God! I made a simple request and you've recited a full-fledged poem. Alright, tell the story the way you want to. But I'll hear the remaining part tomorrow. It's quite late now. Your mother must be worried without you.

Vinay and Sangeeta depart.
The curtain falls.

******

Act-III Scene-I

Time : 2:00 pm.
Location : **Sangeeta's village situated in the foothills of Aravalli.**
On a wall in a coffee shop, there is a painting depicting a solitary person entering a dense jungle in the midst of a fearsome storm. Gazing at it, Sangeeta is transported back to her past. After Sahiram's death, her uncle and aunt began to spread various rumours in the village. Her aunt defamed her more than her uncle. She remembers her mother's words that a dog is the first to bite another dog. She is astonished as to why they still harbour jealousy towards each other. One day, while returning from school, she overhears her aunt talking to some other women.

Sunita : (Sangeeta's aunt) Everyday, I have to encounter that unfortunate woman. First, she devoured her own husband, and even after that, her hunger wasn't satiated; she swallowed my elder brother-in-law. God knows what's coming next. This innocent girl seems to be entering days filled with troubles.

Sangeeta : (Entering that house yelling in anger) Aunt! You have no business to talk about my aunt like that. And please, spare me from your excessive concerns. I know what I need to do. Keep your fake sympathy to yourself.

Sunita	:	You can be as much ill-mannered as you want, but we won't stop thinking good of you. You are naive, we are not.
Sangeeta	:	(Dismissively) I have nothing to do with your hypocritical words. What do you want to prove by sympathizing with those whom you did not come to see when they were alive? You yourself bear a flawed character and you kept blaming my mother. I know you have your eyes fixed on our property.
Sunita	:	(Mockingly) People like you have ruined the meaning of relationships in society. You show as if we've been fed by your father so far. Get lost from here, and stop defending that misfortunate woman.
Sangeeta	:	(Approaching Sunita angrily) Beware of speaking ill about my aunt. Oh, fear just God! Be ashamed of mocking at someone's helplessness.
Sunita	:	Helplessness! Hahaha. What helplessness? What compulsion could the woman be having to destroy another home who had already destroyed one?
Sangeeta	:	I said, have fear. She came here not to settle her own house but ours. She spent day and night taking care of my father.
Sunita	:	I am aware of everything. Had she come here to take care of your father, she wouldn't have married him. Even at this age, she wanted a husband; she could have found someone elsewhere. Why did she victimise my brother-in-law?

Sangeeta	:	(With signs of hatred) Control your filthy thoughts else you will keep wandering aimlessly. Besides, it was not hers but Dad's decision to get married.
Sunita	:	She's a sorceress, a witch. She must have cast a spell on my brother-in-law. Poor man fell her victim.
Sangeeta	:	I'm warning you, Aunt. Now, things won't be good if you utter a single word against my aunt.
Sunita	:	(Looking into Sangeeta's eyes raising her eyebrows) What will you do? Will you harm me, hit me? Your parents were not like that. Who has taught you to be so disrespectful? It's undoubtedly the effect of her necromantic tricks.
Sangeeta	:	Yes, it is necromancy, a sort of magic that has enabled me to cut out the tongue of anyone who speaks ill of my family. If you don't hold your tongue, remember that you won't be able to speak anymore.
Sunita	:	So far, I had been considering you as our family's own child. If you dare lay a hand on me, I will forget all relationships and teach you such a lesson that you will remember for life.
Sangeeta	:	Don't let words like 'family' and 'relationships' come to your dirty tongue. In the past year and a half, all of you have shown your true colours.
Sunita	:	(Looking at the neighbour standing nearby) Have you seen? Such are the

	values of this generation. She doesn't have manners to talk to her elders.
Sangeeta	: People like you have made a joke of sacred word like 'elder'. What kind of values should I learn from people like you? Should I learn to provoke a brother-in-law and get an elder sister-in-law beaten, to fulfil your selfish interests and leave your family members in trouble, to keep an evil eye on the property of others, to treat your husband as nothing, to keep sitting at others' houses all day long and backbiting your own family members or should I learn how to cheat on your husband. If you want to be respected like elders, first put a stop to your petty activities. I feel insulted calling you 'aunt'.
Sunita	: Now, I am sure that she's not just a necromancer, she's a witch also, a witch! But regardless of what happens, I can't let her devour you.
Sangeeta	: (In anger, pushing her bag to the side and giving Sunita a strong shove) I told you not to utter a word about my aunt. Today, I've just pushed you, but if you ever speak about my aunt, my parents, or my family, I'll deface you.

Saying this, Sangeeta picked up her bag and quickly came out of that house.

| Sunita | : (Lying on the ground spreading a poisonous smile on her lips, says to herself) Cheap scoundrel! You don't |

know that you had hurt the ego of a female serpent and you will have to face dire consequences. Fun, hahaha, yes, that's what I am going to have. My real game starts now.

The curtain falls.

******

Act-III Scene-II

Time : 3 pm.
Location : Sangeeta's uncle's house
An offended Sunita comes back home, starts spreading her dangerous trap and provokes her husband.

Sunita : (To her husband) Pay attention to your niece. She talks too much nonsense. She calls me inauspicious just because I don't have children. She was talking about disfiguring my face. I endured it. Had it been someone else in my place, the person would have ruined hers.

Badlu : Your mind is messed up. I've asked you several times not to get involved with her. If you want to use your mind, focus on getting rid of this old lady. After that, we'll take Sannu with us and our work is done. Once we adopt her, all her property will be ours. I've heard that this old lady's father sold all his property and deposited 30-40 lakh rupees in her account.

Sunita : But how long do I have to keep humiliating myself?

Badlu : If you've done it for this long, wait a bit longer. In a year or two, she'll turn eighteen, and then she'll have rights to her father, mother and her aunt's property and accounts. Only then will we implement our plan. We'll have discussion on her marriage. Until then, endure some more bitterness. After all, this property belongs to our family. Why should other people enjoy it? Stay calm, be patient.

With that, Badlu leaves.

Sunita : (To herself) Marriage... well, it's an interesting idea. I need to think about it seriously.

Sonu, Badlu's friend's son, who often helps around the house, enters.

Sonu : What are you thinking, Aunt?

Sunita : Hey, Sonu! When did you sneak through?

Sonu : I came just when Uncle was asking you to calm down. I thought I should not enter. May be something had happened between you two.

Sunita : Nothing happened between us, Sonu. But this girl has caused great problems for us. Your uncle and I are very worried about this.

Sonu : You are right, Aunt. That girl is ill-mannered. One day, when I was coming to your home, I saw her on the way. I just looked at her and she got upset. She humiliated me in the presence of many people. A girl and that too an orphan, people obviously start favouring her. I had to swallow my disgust that day.

Sunita	:	(To herself) So, even this guy is hurt. Good, only the wearer knows where the shoe pinches. (With a wicked smile) Oh! She didn't spare you either.
Sonu	:	Yes, Aunt. This girl bears a twisted mind. We need to fix it. Apart from you, no one else seems to be capable of handling this job.
Sunita	:	(Secretly pleased) This guy is a loaded gun. He'll fire as soon as he's triggered. But first, I should fix the target. Even if this enmity never existed, where would it go? I have a complete dossier on him. (Turning to Sonu) We have nothing to do with her conduct, Sonu. We'll get her married in a year or two. Someone will surely mend her ways. By the way, talking about marriage, there were discussions about your marriage too.
Sonu	:	Yes, Aunt. My parents started discussing about marriage as soon as I completed my diploma in Civil Engineering. But I refused.
Sunita	:	Why? Why did you refuse? Do you have an affair with someone else?
Sonu	:	Leave it, Aunt. Nowadays, it's everyone's business, but not everyone gets a partner of one's choice. Our generation is still in between. Our parents do talk about giving freedom to their children but never truly allow us to choose our partner. What do we call it? "The Generation gap." Yes, this

factor has reached a dangerous point in our time. The elderly generation that has no control over its habits is preaching to the next generations about not following unfair practices.

Sunita : (Raising her eyebrows) You've become quite a philosopher. Well, tell me who is the one that has turned you into such a great philosopher. May I help you in anyway?

Sonu : (With twinkling eyes) Really? Can you help me, Aunt?

Sunita : I'm not joking. Tell me who she is so that I can make a plan.

Sonu : Don't mind, Aunt. I'm crazy about Sangeeta. But looking at her attitude, I don't think she'll marry me. Rather, I feel she hates me terribly.

Sunita's eyes lit up upon hearing Sangeeta's name.

Sunita : (To herself with a hint of being happy) Bravo, my boy! You've hit the jackpot. You have eased out all my difficulties. The well has come right to the doorstep of a thirsty person.

Sonu : (Continuing) What do you think, Aunt? I have done nothing wrong with your niece. It's just one-sided love. Well, in a few days, I'll speak to her anyway. I had planned to talk to her on the very day she humiliated me. But now, I'll talk to her. If she agrees, well and good, otherwise, I'll tell my family to arrange my marriage wherever they want.

Sunita	:	(To herself) Wow! The fire has already started burning. I just need to knead the dough to bake the breads. (Controlling her emotions) Alright, first tell me what job are you doing right now.
Sonu	:	Right now, I'm not employed anywhere but I'm engaged in some part-time job with a friend.
Sunita	:	What kind of business are you doing?
Sonu	:	(Anxiously to himself) She is asking just what shouldn't be asked.
Sunita	:	What are you thinking? Even if you're not doing anything, it's not a big deal. But I met your friend yesterday who works part time with you. One of my friends arranged a meeting with him. He was saying that you're also making good money out of this part time job.
Sonu	:	(Nervous and feeling trapped, asks himself) Oh my goodness! Have I fallen into her trap?
Sunita	:	Why aren't you answering, Sonu? You must know that I'm well aware of what you do in the city. You deceive your father, pretending to have a part-time job. I know your part-time job, Mr. Gigolo. After all, you're so handsome, you should do something worthwhile. Your body and its handsomeness should be used by someone else.
Sonu	:	(Half smiling, half frowning in embarrassment) Sorry, Aunt. Now that you know everything, I'll tell you. Yes,

I work as a gigolo. In today's world, expenses are so high that you have to find alternative ways to earn. There are no jobs, and even if you manage to get one, the salary is barely enough. After spending lakhs on education, an engineer earns just 15-20 thousand rupees a month. Having spent huge money, it's justified that our families pressure us to earn.

Sunita : You mean no good work is left in the world to be done?

Sonu : No, but once while doing diploma in engineering, I spent excessive pocket money with friends. It made me run out of money and I remained hungry for two days. Being left with no alternative, I asked a friend for money. He arranged me a part time job. I had to teach a madam twice or thrice a week and payment was to be made on daily basis. Madam was very rich, she would pay Rs 2000 daily out of which Rs 500 was my friend's commission. I agreed, went happily but later I realized that the matter was different. Still I didn't oppose as it was finding fun and money together at the same place. Debaucheries have the strongest attraction in this world. Once trapped, I could not get out of it. But don't worry, I will give up the idea of marrying Sangeeta.

Sunita : Aren't you ashamed of doing this?

Sonu	:	Shame! For what, aunt? In this world, nearly everyone bears some fault. I once believed our elders were highly principled, upholding strong moral values. However, it's become evident that this was a facade. Each person harbours his own hidden desires, and no one is truly without fault. Everyone is in pursuit of opportunities. I've noticed that all the women who have reached out to me so far are middle-aged, married for a long time, with grown children. Shouldn't they feel ashamed of their actions? What kind of example are they setting for their own kids?
Sunita	:	So, are all women like this? If a woman stays silent, it doesn't mean she's helpless. There's reality covered with her silence. The day her silence breaks, you'll exhaust yourself listing all the cheats and deceivers.
Sonu	:	Leave it, Aunt! When my silence breaks, even those respectable households will be shaken. When did I say that men are innocent? But, it is definitely worth thinking about where the society is headed. Sorry aunty, I am leaving. But I request you not to tell all this to my father. At least a few lotuses are still blooming in the pond filled with mud.
Sunita	:	(To herself) Let you go! How can I let the prey in my hands go so easily? Wow son! When the truth is out you want to

leave. If you had to quit, why did you break into my house? (Controlling herself) Wait Sonu. You must have got angry. I was just saying that you are the child of good parents. You shouldn't have done that. Still don't worry. I have a plan to get you out of this muddy pond. If you follow my plan, you will not only get rid of it but also earn money too. I will talk to Sangeeta. I will convince her. She is arrogant because she possesses a lot of money.

Sonu : Arrogant about money? Where would she even have money? Whatever was there with her family got spent on her parents' illness. If there's a little left, it's probably consumed by that old aunt's sickness.

Sunita : No, this girl is worth millions. She's the sole heir to all her mother, aunt, and father's assets. Her paternal grandfather was very wealthy and had no sons. The entire inheritance was in his daughters' names before their death and now she is the heir of all their wealth and property.

Sonu : Oh! So now I understand the secret of her arrogance. The fable of *Panchatantra* seems to be right that the rat sitting on a treasure jumps excessively.

Sunita : If you marry her, you'll become a millionaire in no time. This dirty business of yours will also be history. But the condition is that I will get half of

	her wealth. Don't tell anyone about me, and I'll keep your part time job a secret.
Sonu	: (To himself) This plan seems interesting, but I should ask her first what my role will be.
Sunita	: What are you thinking? If you don't agree, you can leave.
Sonu	: (As he continues thinking) How can I leave just like that? The plan may be poisonous, but the antidote to poison is poison itself. I will swallow this poison whether I die or recover instantly.
Sunita	: Why have you suddenly turned quiet? If you don't agree to it, you can leave.
Sonu	: But what do I need to do?
Sunita	: Nothing special or new, just what you do every day.
Sonu	: What? With you? You mean you want the same?
Sunita	: (Looking angrily at Sonu) No, don't even think about it. I'm not interested in such things. I'm only desirous of money, only money. Do you understand? I'm talking about Sangeeta.
Sonu	: What? With Sangeeta? How can you even think of that, Aunt? She's not that kind of girl. And she already has issues with me; she won't agree to this, not in my wildest dreams.
Sunita	: You have to do it forcefully. Do you understand? Just do that.
Sonu	: (Surprisingly) Aunt, have you lost your mental balance? You're planning such

disgusting things about your own niece. This won't be possible. Being a gigolo is, perhaps, my compulsion, but being a rapist is not. I have no appetite for sex, nor for money. I'm working part-time for now. The day I go full-time, I'll have plenty of money. How could you even think I'd do something so vile?

Sunita : Look, Sonu, the person who is your boss in the city is my friend's gigolo. We've gathered some photos from him. These gigolos are up for sale. They do anything for money. (Taking an envelope out of her closet) Here you go, have a look at these photos.

Sonu : (After looking at the pictures, with a mix of concern and surprise on his face) But how can all this be done? After committing rape, I'll be behind bars followed by disgrace in society.

Sunita : (With a wicked smile on her twisted lips) Innocent Sonu! You're still a layman. First, hear my whole plan, and then think.

Sonu : (With a combination of worry and astonishment on his face) Alright, tell me, Aunt.

Sunita : Tonight, you'll do it forcefully with Sangeeta. Your uncle and I will catch you red-handed. After that, we'll immediately call a village council meeting in the morning. In the meeting, you'll have to say that you didn't go willingly, but Sangeeta was already in a relationship with you and called you to stay one night with her. When you were caught, she accused you. In the village council, we'll manage both Sangeeta and the council. To settle the dispute, we'll impose the condition that if Sonu is ready to marry Sangeeta, we won't hand him over to the police. As per plan, the council will also coerce Sangeeta into marriage. It's better to enjoy Sangeeta and her property than to come out of those compromising pictures, bringing defame to the entire family and staying unmarried throughout life. Getting you declared innocent by the council is our job.

Sonu : But aunty, after marriage, will she be able to accept a rapist under the pressure of society?

Sunita : Why not? Her mother's concepts of previous birth's karma and their consequences are deeply rooted in her mind. We will remind her the words of her deceased mother. She will consider it as the result of her own past deeds and will become normal in a few months.

(Back in the present)

Sangeeta : (With tears in her eyes) That night that beast came to our house. My aunt and I were sleeping on separate cots in the courtyard. In my sleep he made me smell something which made me unconscious for some time. As soon as he started raping me, my aunt woke up. She picked up a stick lying in the courtyard and hit him in the waist and shouted loudly for help. That brute snatched the stick from aunty and hit on her head. Aunt became unconscious and has been mentally disturbed since then.

Vinay : (Wiping Sangeeta's tears with his handkerchief.) Today respect for you has grown in my mind forever. Now I have decided that I will request God for making you my wife not only for this birth but for as many times as I am born. From today onwards, it is my responsibility to take care of you and deal with your enemies.

Sangeeta : There is no need for that. Aunty and I did not succumb to the pressure of the *Panchayat*. Uncle and aunt put pressure on me to bury the family matters at home. The *Panchayat* gave us two days' time, but during these two days, I called a police inspector, a friend of my father, and told him everything. That scoundrel and my uncle and aunt were arrested by the police. After this incident, we sold our property from the village and came to live in the city where my Dad's policeman friend supported us. We came to know about this whole conspiracy later when the police unfolded it. Due to so much tension, I could not clear civil service exams but after working hard, I became an engineer and independent as well. Aunty got a lot of treatment but she could not recover completely. I will live with this guilt throughout my life that it's me who is responsible for my aunt's condition.

Saying this, Sangeeta started crying bitterly. Vinay wiped her tears, asked her to get up and both of them walked hand in hand towards Vinay's car.
The curtain falls.

******

Act-III Scene-III

Time : 9 am
Location : Sangeeta's father's friend Police Inspector Avtar Singh's house in Jaipur city.
Sangeeta had finished her story, but Vinay wasn't satisfied with just the tale of her hardships. He also wanted to know if there was goodness in the world which helps in overcoming the negative effects of hatred developed towards society. He wanted to know how the negative feelings in Sangeeta could be purged out. Sangeeta's story now takes him to Jaipur, where she left the evil behind, and she found goodness in the form of a police officer. Sangeeta's father's police friend and his wife are sitting at home in the lawn.

Sangeeta	:	Uncle, how will I ever repay the favour you've done for us? You've come into my life like an angel.
Avtar Singh	:	Don't say that, dear? I didn't do any favour for you. Your father told me about you before he passed away, but I was so occupied with work that I couldn't get in touch. It's a good thing that day you didn't accept the village council's decision and called me; otherwise, I couldn't have forgiven myself for a lifetime.
Sangeeta	:	Uncle, you don't know. By rescuing us

		from that hellish place, you've done a tremendous favour to both of us.
Avtar Singh	:	No one does anyone a favour. There is an ultimate truth in the universe that there is always light at the end of a tunnel.
Sangeeta	:	But Uncle, we were lost in such a desolate wilderness, where there seemed to be no way out and where ferocious wild animals were always looking for a chance to attack us.
Avtar Singh	:	Every hardship we face in life bears hidden lessons, my dear.
Sangeeta	:	But uncle, the circumstances in our time are teaching us something entirely different. Incidents like looting, addiction, theft, deceit, murder, and rape have negatively impacted the youth's minds. You being a police officer probably understand this better than anyone else.
Avtar Singh	:	That's true; we do deal with all the evils of society. Yet, we continue to live with the hope that things will change. Circumstances are never the same forever.
Sangeeta	:	In what hope should we live, Uncle? Here, even our elders, who are supposed to provide us security, conspire to tarnish our reputation. You were our saviour; otherwise, I would have been ruined.
Avtar Singh	:	It's destiny's will, my child. I didn't do

anything. Still, I'll say this much – more attachment brings more pain. Everyone has to fight their own battles.

Sangeeta : How should I fight, Uncle? I don't understand whether survival depends on skills or cunningness.

Avtar Singh : Skills always matter. If you assess the time and circumstances, you'll realize that the power of cunningness is time bound.

Sangeeta : The circumstances are totally unfavourable, Uncle. We have entered an era where society remains silent on the brutal murder of innocent girls who fight for their dignity while applauding a porn star on social or public platforms. The deteriorating level of entertainment is representative of our deteriorating mind-set. What message are we leaving behind for the coming generations?

Avtar Singh : Your anger is both personal and justified, my child. Just as artificial laughter is a blend of deception and cunningness, anger and truth also have an alliance. Every incident or accident has two sides. If the police and investigative agencies only see one side, there won't be a proper solution to any problem.

Sangeeta : So, are you also in favour of glorifying wrongdoing?

Avtar Singh : Not at all. Committing sins all of the days and going to the temple in the weekend can't help getting rid of the consequences of sins. The principle of punishment should give way to the importance of reformation. If someone has the will to reform, he should seek redemption and penance like Valmiki, Ajamil, and Angulimal, rather than taking refuge in social or public platforms.

Sangeeta : Then why aren't such activities stopped? Body trade is a much better business than engaging in shameless acts through these public and social platforms. At least this way, society won't receive a wrong message. If there is a genuine desire for reform, what can be the better way to start the journey of reform than rescuing and uplifting the girls trapped in this muck and dedicating entire life for their welfare?

Avtar Singh : Your anger won't bring any change, my dear, because there are more admirers of shamelessness than values. Still you need not worry; the truth may be obscure, but it's not destructible.

Sangeeta : Uncle, the truth may be imperishable, but it doesn't necessarily remain in happy state.

Avtar Singh : I know that you are going to lead an exceptionally good and content life, my child. Nature bestows as much happiness as it does sorrow upon those who undergo immense hardships.

Sangeeta : My perspective is different, Uncle. If, after enduring suffering, happiness is

		inevitable, what is the use of the skills acquired during difficult times in life?
Avtar Singh	:	Sangeeta, you're thinking just as I used to think. My father went through a lot of difficulties, and during those days, he used to take me to a saint. I asked the same question to that saint.
Sangeeta	:	Really? What answer did the saint give?
Avtar Singh	:	The saint explained that competence doesn't solely revolve around confronting evil; the ability to steer clear of it is a skill in itself. Hardships and challenging days equip us with the tools to carve out our distinctive path and serve as a model for generations to come. Every experience holds value. During prosperous times, various temptations exert a stronger pull on us, and it's precisely then that these acquired skills become our saviours.
Sangeeta	:	But if everyone just thinks about themselves, then who will eradicate the world's evil, Uncle?
Avtar Singh	:	Even the creator couldn't eliminate it. Ram came, Krishna came, Buddha came, Mahavir came, sages, saints, enlightened beings and thousands of reformers came, but evil continues to exist. Yes, it can be eliminated only by a person, and that is ourselves and for that, the hardest times are the most appropriate means.
Sangeeta	:	Evil will only be eradicated, Uncle, when

		there is peace in life. And this peace seems almost impossible. There must be some way to establish it, right, Uncle?
Avtār Singh	:	Peace perhaps comes after death. That's why there's a trend of chanting 'Om Shanti' after someone passes away.
Sangeeta	:	After death? What's the use then? Who would know if there's peace? And even if there is, it's only for the one who's passed away.
Avtār Singh	:	There is a place where peace is found, deeply embedded in our culture. Nonetheless, it's essential to be aware that even in the core of goodness, the termites of evil persist. Turbulence is a fundamental aspect of the universe. Therefore, we are consistently instructed to follow the path of peace.
Sangeeta	:	But, uncle, to combat evil, you need the help of a living being. What can be expected from the deceased?
Avtār Singh	:	The deceased can't be ignored, my child. Life and death both provide their teachings. This world is merely an illusion. In this place, nobody will be impacted by someone's life or death. Modern individuals are not like a pair of storks in which, if one is killed by a hunter, the other will suffer deeply and die in agony, and a witness like Valmiki will compose an epic about it. What significance does one's death hold for those relatives who are determined to

	harm them while they are alive?
Sangeeta	: If nobody cares, what can one learn from his death, uncle? And then, what values are left behind for relationships?
Avtār Singh	: Death certainly imparts a universal lesson, reminding us that in the journey of life, a definite end is inevitable, and it may not align with our desires. As far as the significance of relationship is concerned, which relationship are you referring to, my dear? A husband revered as divine by his wife and a father whom children look up to as their role model have now turned into an alcoholic, a gambler, and a debauchee. People are akin to an elephant displaying separate tusks for the audience and tearing them apart. A puppet operated by strings of greed and avarice, he claims that he does everything for his children. This is called hypocrisy.
Sangeeta	: There aren't mistakes made by men alone. You've dealt with cases like Sonu the gigolo. Women are equally responsible for turning a man into a libertine. I think, behind this, modernity is a significant factor, Uncle.
Avtar Singh	: Every age is a modern age in itself. An analyst, centuries after a particular era, re-evaluates it based on current circumstances and reclassifies it accordingly. So, blaming the times is unjust. And yes, I never said that the root of the crime is

	always in one party. When analysing a crime, we the policemen consider both sides: how much of it is within the criminal and how much is there in the victim.
Sangeeta	: If the entire society is corrupt, it implies that it will never change.
Avtar Singh	: In my opinion, the answer lies in the upbringing. Habits change, but not the values inculcated through upbringing. Circumstantial biases change with the change in circumstances, but the vices in blood go from generation to generation. That's why, in Indian culture, a program of character development begins before birth, I mean, the rituals start from the womb of a mother.
Sangeeta	: Uncle, who will teach these values to the upcoming generations? People like you are rare, and if a few exist, who listens to them?
Avtar Singh	: There's no greater teacher nor school than life's experiences. What those challenging circumstances have taught you, no book could have taught. Now it's your responsibility to preserve that learning so that it can be an example for the present and future generations. Remember, the ideals won't be created just by what you say. The learnings will become ideals when you act upon them and demonstrate them in your life.
Sangeeta	: Uncle, even my mother was cultured,

but there was never peace at home. So what's the use of following such cultural practices?

Avtar Singh : When I speak of embracing pure Indian culture, I don't mean it's only for one person to adopt. It is for every individual. Accepting pure Indian culture doesn't mean adhering to one's heart alone; it means adhering to the heart of every person. The peace of one heart doesn't guarantee peace for the entire universe. So, I recommend that every individual should learn this peace mantra from the Yajurveda-

Oṃ dyauḥ śāntirantarikṣaṃ śāntiḥ
pṛthivī śāntirāpaḥ śāntiroṣadhayaḥ śāntiḥ
vanaspatayaḥ śāntirviśvedevāḥ śāntirbrahma śāntiḥ
sarvaṃ śāntiḥ śāntireva śāntiḥ sā mā śāntiredhi
oṃ śāntiḥ śāntiḥ śāntiḥ ||

In other words, "Oh Lord! May there be peace in the heavenly realms, peace in the entire sky, peace on Earth, peace in the waters, peace in the plants and trees, peace in the animals, and peace in all the deities. May I attain the ultimate peace of the Supreme. Om, peace, peace, peace.

Sangeeta : Whose profound thoughts are these, Uncle? A prayer of peace for the entire universe. You seem to be talking about a utopian city that exists nowhere.

Avtar Singh	:	It's obvious that it had been the thinking of a man. When my neighbour's house is not peaceful, there's no significance to peace in my home. If the nation is in chaos, there's no importance of peace in my home. "Vasudhaiva Kutumbakam" (the world is one family) is impossible without "Sarvam Shanti" (peace for all), and "Sarvam Shanti" is meaningless without "Sarve Bhavantu Sukhinah" (may all be happy). Our sages and teachers gave these small principles for the welfare of humanity, but unfortunately, they seem to have been lost over time.
Sangeeta	:	Why is it that good things always seem to be lost, Uncle?
Avtar Singh	:	That, my child, is a kind of illusion created by nature. Perhaps there's some flaw in human thinking. There is an attraction in the physical world that breeds greed and several other vices. The unnecessary accumulation of wealth implies that someone's right will certainly be violated. When these faults come into existence, they continue into the next generation. If they are not stopped, a person succumbs to their own desires and thereby harms his own status.
Sangeeta	:	Then, it must have serious consequences.
Avtar Singh	:	The tree of ambition bears the fruit of ego. Stealing someone's right and giving it to the undeserving leads to a

Mahabharata. Apart from the *Vedic* and the *Mahabharata* eras, such teachings have been provided by saints, gurus, and teachers from time to time. But desire is a natural inclination. These are hardly controlled.

Sangeeta : If desire leaves a person helpless, what's the point of blaming a man, Uncle?

Avtar Singh : You're right, my child. A common man thinks like that only. Our life is worse than insects filled with temptations and distractions.

Sangeeta : But, Uncle, it doesn't seem like you've answered my question.

Avtar Singh : My point is that desires are the root cause. A moth is drawn to the light and burns itself to death but another moth does not learn a lesson and does the same thing. But, dear, humans have been blessed by the Lord with the tool of intellect which can tear out the veil of ignorance and take wisdom out of it. Yet, despite knowing this, the fool continues to move towards his destruction rapidly.

Sangeeta : So, does that mean one has to become a warrior to fight against all these vices?

Avtar Singh : Not a warrior, my child, but one has to become a renunciant. Renunciation is the only solution to this problem.

Sangeeta : You mean one should go to the forests away from the world, uncle.

Avtar Singh : A *Sanyasi* doesn't escape but stays.

> The profound wilderness lies within, wherein man himself is lost. His primary battle is the quest to discover his true self. A *Sanyasi* doesn't stand on the borders of a state waiting for a battle; he recognizes that an ongoing war exists within each moment. Ignorance, vices, temptations, falsehood, and other biases act as relentless armies, persistently invading the domain of our minds in pursuit of capturing our very soul.

Sangeeta : But uncle, these things can also be done by one living a mundane, homely life. What is the need to become a *Sanyasi*?

Avtar Singh : The meaning of *Sannyas* (renunciation) is not staying away from the world, but it's about distancing oneself from ignorance. For this, there is no need to go to a jungle and perform austerities, but one can attain *Sannyas* by living as a householder and burning the fire of knowledge within by doing prescribed duties, thereby incinerating their faults.

Sangeeta : If that's the case, why do people become saints and holy men?

Avtar Singh : This is a part of our culture, my child. It is certain that the end of life is ordained, and so the last phase of life is designated for this purpose.

Sangeeta : But why, Uncle? In that phase, a person should provide the benefit of his experience to their family by living with them. Why should someone become a *Sanyasi*?

Avtar Singh : This is a narrow perspective, dear. By the time they get to that stage their kids should gain wisdom and require no support from them. In that phase of life, the whole world becomes a family. The other reason for this is that, by the time one reaches the second half of life, many of the world's shortcomings are attached to his mind. To shed them off one also needs *Sanyas*. To contemplate your good by ensuring the welfare of all is also a form of *Sanyas*.

Sangeeta : Now, I have got it, Uncle. But I have some more questions in my mind. If you don't mind, may I ask a few more questions?

Avtar Singh : Please ask without hesitation. I also have a daughter, and by God's grace, she's leading a happy life. But looking at your determination, I sometimes wish you were my own daughter.

Sangeeta : Uncle, my heart also wishes you were my father. But now, you can consider me your own daughter and tell me, why aren't the police as good as you?

Avtar Singh : The police are indeed very good, dear, but it's the police personnel who are not up to the mark. There are many reasons for them being not up to the mark, like witnessing an excessive amount of corruption in society, having an overload of work, dealing with a corrupt system, not being able to give time to their children, and enduring the pressure from their superiors. One corrupt police officer can damage the enthusiasm of several good police officers.

Sangeeta : So, is this an incurable disease?

Avtar Singh : No, it's not incurable at all. If society improves, then there won't be any need for the police. The uniform carries power, but if one doesn't learn how to control that power properly, it will be detrimental to both oneself and others. Many police officers are making this mistake. Besides good training for the police, politics and bureaucracy also need reformation. Blaming individual police officers alone is not fair.

Sangeeta : So, the police will never improve?

Avtar Singh : As long as honesty is punished, and dishonesty is rewarded, there won't be any improvement. An honest person, whose only source of livelihood is his job, cannot bear to see their honesty being a problem to their job.

Sangeeta : So, are you saying that one should become dishonest and corrupt in order to save his job?

Avtar Singh : No, that's not what I mean. Sahiram had many shortcomings, but he wasn't dishonest. He also had to suffer the consequences within the system. He faced frequent transfers, superiors gave him a hard time, delayed promotions, and his personal record was tarnished. But he had a remarkable ability to endure losses. Had he not been infected with the deadly disease of suspicion, he would have been a unique person.

Sangeeta : Uncle, if I clear the Civil Services exams and become an IPS officer in future, will I get a chance to reform the system?

Avtar Singh : Most of the opportunities are usually there to derail a person's life, and they are quite attractive. Opportunities which reform either man or society have to be created by our determination. An IPS officer is not an ordinary police officer. He has a significant say in various situations. There have been several occasions when he has taught a lesson to several corrupt and dishonest officers and politicians. I'm pleased that you're advancing your goals with such positive thinking. Nature and the divine will surely support you in this noble endeavour.

Sangeeta : Yes, Uncle, your blessings mean a lot. This is my third year of engineering, and I'm thinking of joining a coaching centre soon.

Avtar Singh : That's a great plan. I'll help you find a good coaching centre. By the time I get one for you, you should strengthen your resolve. Coaching isn't just

		about focused study; it also helps you understand your own situation. You learn from the environment as well.
Sangeeta	:	Thank you, Uncle. I hope I haven't wasted too much of your time today. I apologize for my persistence. Now, may I have your permission to leave?
Avtar Singh	:	No, dear, you haven't wasted any time. Our conversation was like a good *Satsang* (spiritual discourse). I'm glad that God has given me the opportunity to calm your curiosity. Now, go home; your mom must be waiting for you.
Sangeeta	:	Thanks again, Uncle.

Sangeeta departs
The curtain falls.

******

Act-IV Scene-I

Time- 8:30 am
Location- Jeevan's Home in Uttam Nagar, New Delhi.
Jeevan's son Kunal has got married. Kunal and his wife Anju work in separate offices. Anju is ready to go to the office.

Jeevan	:	Anju, are you going to the office?
Anju	:	Yes, Dad, I am running a little late today. I'm just about to leave.
Jeevan	:	Oh, dear, don't take it otherwise, you could have dressed a little better for the office.
Anju	:	Papa, I don't know what happens to you every morning. You always seem to spoil my mood when I am going to office. Today, you've commented on my clothes for the fifth time in a month.
Jeevan	:	Oh dear, I was just saying that. I didn't mean to upset you.
Anju	:	Don't you see anything beyond my clothes? In your time, women used to wear veils. Should I wear a veil while driving to my office?
Jeevan	:	I didn't mean that, my child. I'm not criticizing you. I'm just trying to say that there's a little difference between bachelor life and married life.

Anju : Just keep your vision clear and I'll handle the rest. And yes, if you can't see me going to the office, you might as well stay in your room, but don't comment on my clothes every day.

Kunal, Anju's husband, enters

Kunal : Why are you getting so heated? Don't you have the courtesy to speak respectfully with the elders?

Anju : Courtesy! Is that something only children need to learn? Maybe you should teach your dad a bit too. He keeps making comments on my clothes every day. Can't I even wear clothes of my choice? Doesn't he see anything else beyond my body?

Kunal : Why do you always interpret everything conversely? If he's said something, he must have thought it through before saying it.

Anju : Why is his thinking limited to clothes only? Why doesn't he see my competence, my struggle?

Kunal : Don't take everything negatively. If he has said something, there must be some good intention behind it, either for your sake or the family's.

Anju : Wow, really? So, it means I'm the one who doesn't see what's good for me and the family. Today, we have a cultural program in the office. The boss asked me to be the anchor, and your dad is making comments about my clothes.

I know that there's a generation gap between him and me. But he must know how hard it is to get a job in today's world. Should I put my career at stake for him? I'm leaving. I don't have much time, and I don't want to stay in this house anymore. Either he or I will stay here. In a day or two, I'll look for a different place to live. We will shift there.

Anju leaves, and Jeevan and his wife look at each other.

Jeevan : (To Jyoti) It seems like our days in this house are over.

Kunal : (After Anju's departure) Dad, I know. Probably, your intentions were right. But I think, in this matter, you should stay quiet. The culture in Anju's office is like that only. She's not the only one who wears such dress. All the girls there come dressed like that. And people should wear what makes them look good.

Jeevan : But son...

Kunal : But what, Dad? Nowadays, this is the culture. Despite a dress code in the government offices, your office girls also sometimes wear modern clothes. Have you ever reprimanded them for it? No. So, why worry unnecessarily? It's just a generation gap. It's a transitional phase. We need to accept it.

Jeevan : Son, I don't have a problem with her dress. These days, I'm more concerned

	about the unsafe environment. Gangs of hooligans hang around every corner. If someone does something mischievous, it can lead to trouble.
Kunal	: Dad, you're worrying unnecessarily. If a girl can give such a strong response to you, do you think she'll stay quiet on the comments from the hoodlums on street? Nowadays, girls are empowered enough to respond effectively to any ill-treatment or violence.
Jeevan	: Yes, son, I've seen that very well today. And I also realized that if I keep talking too much, it could have dire consequences. I've seen examples of the misuse of power, especially after the women's empowerment phase. I'll find a solution to your concerns by this evening. You may go to your office without any worries.
Kunal	: Why are you so much worried, Dad? You took Anju's words to heart. In the evening we will sit and talk. When she comes back from the office, you will find her smiling. You will do nothing, we will all stay together.

Kunal leaves for the office. Jeevan's wife Jyoti, who has been silently listening, sits down in a chair. She has forgotten that Jeevan also has to go to the office. Among the three who leave for office, Jeevan is the last because his office is the closest. Jyoti appears worried, and Jeevan approaches her.

Jeevan	: Don't worry, dear. I'll resolve your concerns by this evening. Both of us are

healthy and can take care of ourselves. We will manage to cook for us. If it becomes too difficult, I'll hire a maid for you. We can't stay here anymore. I've received calls from Anju's dad twice. He was indirectly threatening me that if I don't stop bothering Anju, he'll take action. Nowadays, parents don't see their children's mistakes. If they complain even a little, both my job and Kunal's peace will be at stake. My son is decent, so I can't interfere in his life. Pack my lunch; I'm going to work now.

Jyoti : I have no problem with these clothes either. But it's essential to dress according to the occasion and the place. What kind of an era have we entered? There's no culture or cultural love left. Clothing is becoming more westernized, and the behaviour is worse than uncivilized. The education this girl has received was completed by me 25-26 years ago. I've been to London with you a couple of times. People there might wear shorter clothes, but their thinking is broad. No street group of rowdy boys bothers a passing girl. It feels like revealing clothing is worn here only to invite the unruly boys.

Jeevan : I feel that the time doesn't agree with you or me. In between every two generations, there comes a transitional period that creates issues for both the

	generations. Perhaps the art of living is hidden in it.
Jyoti	: There's a difference between openness and nudity. The veil was unjust, not allowing girls to get education was wrong, denying them equal opportunities was unfair, and not treating them as humans was an injustice. But is talking so indelicately a form of civilized behaviour?
Jeevan	: What's the use of thinking without reason? Your truth is truth only for your generation. Today's truth is something else; accept it. The most destructive consequence of giving up your culture and embracing another is that relationships lose their meaning.
Jyoti	: It's so strange that all your NRI friends' wives ask us to send them traditional sarees, and our daughters prefer Western dresses. There's nothing wrong with the clothes; it's the low thinking of people...
Jeevan	: (Interrupting) You mean it's my thinking that's below the mark?
Jyoti	: Why jump to conclusions without letting me finish? My point is that every time, place, and culture have their own attire that adds to the grace.
Jeevan	: This is what I was also trying to say that shoes are made for the feet and a turban is meant for the head. I have no aversion to English clothing. A *Sherwani* and a

	bride's attire cannot be worn every day. I also wear English clothes, but I never transgress the boundaries of my culture. I have never disgraced my father's traditional attire while wearing a shirt and pants.
Jyoti	: Today's generation never understands this point. Clothes should not be associated with knowledge or wisdom; however, they must be linked with culture. In today's era, manners are reflected through both clothing and behaviour. This generation doesn't comprehend that mere clothes are not the proof of being well-educated.
Jeevan	: What can we do, dear? Who gives value to the values? While accomplishing their mission, Dr. B. R. Ambedkar, C. V. Raman, Jagdish Chandra Basu, Vikram Sarabhai, A. P. J. Abdul Kalam, and Chandrayaan's scientists also wore western clothes but they never turned uncivilized.
Jyoti	: We were enjoying good time. Who knew that such bad times would come all of a sudden? Is leaving home the only solution to this?
Jeevan	: At the moment, no solution seems to be appropriate. Both of us will have to support each other. If we don't do that, our child's life will become a living hell.
Jyoti	: What guarantee is there that after we leave home, she will let our child live

	peacefully? A woman understands another woman's mentality better. If there is no control or restrictions, the problem will only increase. Freedom doesn't mean being unruly. Besides, even Kunal wants us to stay here.
Jeevan	: (In a serious tone) I know you have had more experiences than me, but what I have seen in the outside world is quite horrifying. Achieving progress often requires crossing various moral boundaries. Both men and women are involved in this. For now, the only path to peace seems to be separation. I should also say that we are not perfect either.
Jyoti	: Use this dialogue on yourself. I'm perfectly fine. I've never opposed your decisions before but I might not have wholeheartedly accepted them. However, today I'll have to draw a line between my motherhood and wifely duties. My heart will remain here, but my body will go with you. (She becomes emotional) I got stuck in between, neither of this side nor of that. Well leave it, you are late for your office. Let me quickly pack your tiffin.

After saying this, Jyoti heads towards the kitchen.
The curtain falls.

******

Act-IV Scene-II

Time- 6:30 p.m
Location – Ramesh's house in Uttam Nagar, New Delhi.
Both Ramesh and Vinay have reached home from their office. Vinay has come back home after five days. On one side, Vinay and Manju are sitting on the sofa in the guest room and Ramesh is sitting very restless on the other. No one speaks anything for a while. Finally, Ramesh breaks his silence to vent his anger out.

Ramesh : I'd heard that nothing can overpower love, but I never thought that someone would disrespect his father in the name of love.

Vinay : Dad, I didn't do anything to disrespect you. After getting promotion, it was my first day in the office, and I had to take charge of several new responsibilities. That's why I had to go to the office. But as soon as I reached the office, my boss sent me on a five-day business trip.

Ramesh : Well done, my son! Only you've gotten a job, and just you've been promoted. We are just humble labourers. There's no such thing as promotions in our line of work.

Vinay : I didn't mean that, Dad. You always misinterpret everything.

Ramesh	:	Your tongue behaves like scissors. I'm a proven fool. I kept expecting values and manners from today's generation. I had forgotten that you're earning now and have become independent. So, I should present myself respectfully before you.
Vinay	:	(With a lowered head) Sorry, Dad. If my words are taken negatively and cause trouble at home, I will remain silent.
Ramesh	:	Listen carefully, son. Undoubtedly, this is your father's house, but how could you forget that only your father's rules apply in your father's home? If you want to live in the way you like, first build your own house. Get lost from here tomorrow morning.

After hearing this, Vinay silently walks away to another room.

Manju	:	Why are you so harsh to our son? Meet that girl once. She might be just like what you want. Vinay accepts all your words. You should also accept his choices.
Ramesh	:	(Angrily) How insistent will you be for this ill-mannered boy? I'm respected in society. My colleagues in office respect me. I can't risk my reputation.
Manju	:	If she's good, then what's the harm in bringing her to our home?
Ramesh	:	You're blind to reason. You can't see anything. After marriage, she'll bring her ill mother here. Then we'll have to take care of her too. She's not just looking for a husband; she's also searching for a caregiver for her ill and

elderly mother. The girl has played a smart game. She's cunning and sly. Tell him that I won't accept that girl under any circumstances.

Manju : What if he doesn't agree?

Ramesh : Then tell him that he will have to leave our house tomorrow.

Manju : Your stubbornness will destroy this family.

Ramesh : Destruction, both of your actions will lead to it. It's all the consequence of your favouritism that today he dared to speak up to me. Now, I can't bear it even for a moment. He must leave this home.

Manju : What I endured, I won't let my child endure. Listen to my decision also, if he goes, I'll go with him. Stay alone in this house and keep talking to these walls.

Ramesh : Yes, go for sure. Get lost. Your undue support has spoilt him. I sacrificed day and night for you people. I compromised my health for this family. You all ate hot meals, and I had cold ones. But how could I know that he'd foster on my food and sing someone else's praises? Live two days away from home, and you all will regain your senses.

Manju : Fed him? Have you raised your son or a slave? Even a pet animal isn't treated with such cruelty. Enough is enough, now I won't endure any abuse, neither on myself nor on my son.

Ramesh	:	(In anger, grabbing Manju's hand and pushing her out) Shameless woman! You dare to threaten me in my own house! Get out of here right now.
Vinay	:	(Running from the other room and holding his mother) Don't you have any shame, assaulting my mother? Who will wait for the next morning, we are leaving this place right now. (Turning to his mother) Come on, Mom, it's better to live in a rented house.
Ramesh	:	Yes, yes, get lost now. You've enjoyed beneath your father's shelter until today. You'll understand the real life now. Get out of here, right now.

Vinay and Manju depart with their belongings.
The curtain falls.

******

Act-IV Scene-III

Time- 07:30 am
Location – A big mall in Gurugram.
Vinay and Sangeeta have had a court marriage. Both are living in a rented flat with Vinay and Sangeeta's mother. It has been a month since the marriage. Today is a holiday and both of them have come to visit the mall.

Sangeeta	:	It's been a month since we got married. So much has changed in this one month. I'm feeling guilty.
Vinay	:	Guilty, for what? What wrong have you done?
Sangeeta	:	I should have sacrificed my happiness and handed my life over to the circumstances.
Vinay	:	Then you should have made all the decisions yourself. Why did you let me intervene?
Sangeeta	:	I am in between. Neither here nor there. My relatives have abandoned me, and now I don't have the courage to face yours.
Vinay	:	You don't need to be so disheartened. We are living in a time where almost all relationships have either lost their significance or are on the verge of doing so.

Sangeeta	:	So, should we turn barbarian? How can life go on without relationships? Are we living together without any relationships?
Vinay	:	What will you achieve by holding onto lifeless relationships? You're already carrying a lot of burden, how much more will you bear? Some relationships, where there is no vitality, should be let go of for a while.
Sangeeta	:	You have never been so detached? What has suddenly happened to you?
Vinay	:	Yes, today, river Ganga of *Guru Ravidas Ji* has got a reverse flow. Before today, you used to be engaged in philosophy, and today I'm doing the same job.
Sangeeta	:	But why? What has happened today?
Vinay	:	Nothing, the Nature has taught a lesson that in this heartless world, emotions hold no value. Mistakes are committed by the elders and the punishment is accorded to the younger.
Sangeeta	:	I don't agree with that. Even though my elders didn't treat me well, I still believe that if it were really like that, we wouldn't be sitting together today.
Vinay	:	Your agreement or disagreement doesn't matter. This truth is found across history, from the epics to the Vedas and even today, it has been evident. Ram went to exile due to Dasharath's mistake, the war of *Mahabharat* happened because of Dhritarashtra's ambition and Bheesh-

	ma's fierce vow, and Ravan's arrogance led to the destruction of great warriors like Kumbhakarna and Meghnath. What other examples do you want?
Sangeeta	: Everything has two sides, Vinay. Avtar uncle had once told a profound thing that nothing happens in vacuum. There is always a valid reason behind every small or big happening. That's the rule of this world.
Vinay	: Do you really consider yourself a part of this world? What misconception are you living in, madam? We've broken the world's law and order long back. If we hadn't, we would have ceased to live together.
Sangeeta	: You shouldn't think so negatively.
Vinay	: I've seen it being extremely emotional. Nothing productive has come out of it so far. Take away all my emotions and bring, if you can, 100 grams of roasted grams in exchange. We'll make *Chaat* out of them and enjoy eating together.
Sangeeta	: Don't you think that Papa might be feeling distressed alone over there?
Vinay	: What difference does it make whether I think so or not? He should feel it too.
Sangeeta	: Shut up, Vinay! You're crossing all limits of courtesy. Just consider that he is your father, and he has the right to make some decisions in your life. My parents have treated us very badly, but we never gave up values.

Vinay	:	We didn't leave the home. He kicked us not only out of the house but also out of his life. Now, let him live his life in the way he likes. Sangeeta, the major flaw in ego is that it distances us from everyone.
Sangeeta	:	Granted that ego has veiled his intelligence, but think for a moment, aren't you doing the same? Everyone gets angry once in a while. Imagine if you were in their place, what would you do?
Vinay	:	I would never kick my wife and child out. I would never be so arrogant to say that this is my house, and only my decisions will prevail here. I never insist on auctioning my child for dowry.
Sangeeta	:	Every situation has two sides. In this situation, we are victims, but when such a situation, like your parents, arises with us only then I will try to understand the depth and value of these words. Try thinking this way once, Vinay. Who is evil whether a person or time?
Vinay	:	So, will you also auction our future children for dowry?
Sangeeta	:	Absolutely not. How can you think such a thing about me?
Vinay	:	I've been trying to make you understand this for so long. Having children and raising them is not our compulsion, rather, it's our choice for our happiness. Will you ever tell your own children

	that you did them a favour by raising them?
Sangeeta	: Such a day will never come. The mistakes for which we are paying will never be repeated in case of our children.
Vinay	: That's the problem. If the coming generations decide that they will not repeat the mistakes of the previous generations, then the world will indeed improve. But unfortunately, that never happens.
Sangeeta	: Change comes crawling. Why do you see the entire world through the same lens? Good people live here as well.
Vinay	: Yes, madam. I've also read a bit of history and literature. Ram was good, he went to the forest and had to ultimately take self-immolation. Krishna was good, he had to leave behind Gokul, cows, Radha, and his flute, and was killed by a *Bheel*. Pandavas were good, their rights were snatched away, Draupadi was dishonoured, they had to spend time in exile, beg, and face a terrible war, and in the end, they left everything prematurely. Sometimes, being good seems to be a bad thing.
Sangeeta	: That's just one side of the coin. If Ram hadn't gone to the forest, what would have happened to Ahilya, Sabri, Hanuman, and Sugriva? Tadaka, Khara, Dushana, Bali, and other villains, how would they have been punished?

Vinay	:	Okay, I understand. But please tell me, Shri Shri Sangeet Das Ji Maharaj, why Pandavas had to go into exile if, unlike Ram, they had no extraordinary tasks to perform? Why did they endure such hardships?
Sangeeta	:	(Smiling as Vinay addressed her as 'Maharaj') I've had a detailed discussion with Avtar uncle on both the great epics. I also agree on one point that one who gambles away one's property and even one's wife in a game of dice should be treated even worse than what they faced.
Vinay	:	But all of that was done by Yudhishthir alone; what was the fault of the other four Pandavas and Draupadi?
Sangeeta	:	(With anger on her face) Doing injustice is not the only sin; tolerating injustice is also a sin. If putting a question mark on the decision of the elder brother is against morality, then silently witnessing your own wife being staked like a commodity is both cowardice and a grave sin. Their exile wasn't wrong in any sense. And for Draupadi, was it necessary to cross all moral boundaries and say, "Blind son of a blind man?"
Vinay	:	(To himself) She is acquiring the form of *Chandi*. Hopefully, she won't take me on. (Controlling himself) Forgive me, *Devi*. Please calm down. My intention was not to make you angry.

Sangeeta : (With a slight smile) I'm not angry, Vinay. But what bothers me is that people interpret epics according to their convenience. I never wish such foolish mistakes from a learned and wise husband like you. Just as a coin has two sides, the world doesn't run on a single force but is balanced by two opposing forces.

Vinay : (With a long sigh) Thank God, I am safe! I am pleased that you consider me wise. But, Devi, why regret if the balance is maintained? Problems arise when the balance is disturbed. Balance is not created from one side but from both sides.

Sangeeta : This is what I have been trying to explain for so long. Don't create an imbalance in your home because of me.

Vinay : Why do you always drag yourself in between? I've said it before, it's not you, but his own thoughts that trouble him.

Sangeeta : I'm not bringing myself in between. I was on the edge, but yes, for a few days, I've definitely come between you and your father. Who knows what will happen now?

Vinay : Don't we have any rights? Can't we live our lives in our own way?

Sangeeta : Don't even talk about rights, Vinay. These ears can't bear it anymore. Since I have grown wise, I've been pulling with my own hands the cart overloaded with

		my duties. I don't even know if there are any rights for me.
Vinay	:	Do you doubt my love, or have you lost trust on my abilities?
Sangeeta	:	I've never trusted even God as much as I trust you. If I tell you the truth, after the tragic episode at my home, I had decided not to get married. But your pure soul, sweet words, commitment to justice, and selflessness are so transparent that even a blind person couldn't doubt your love and abilities. I'm just thinking about what society will say.
Vinay	:	So, are you afraid of society?
Sangeeta	:	Not afraid of society but of my fate that has been chasing me for years.
Vinay	:	I want to fight with your fate, Sangeeta. Why don't you understand this?
Sangeeta	:	No, I won't let you do that. My actions, my destiny, and the punishment are all mine to bear. Why should someone else interfere?
Vinay	:	So now, I'm someone else? Have we been acting out a drama of love so far?
Sangeeta	:	I didn't say that.
Vinay	:	Then what do you mean by saying this?
Sangeeta	:	Meanings have lost their significance, Vinay. There is so much injustice and cruelty everywhere that the whole world seems senseless now.
Vinay	:	I exist in the same world too.
Sangeeta	:	What do you know about what you mean to me?

Vinay	:	(Looking into Sangeeta's eyes) So, madam, tell me then. Let me know my place.
Sangeeta	:	(Holding Vinay's hand and looking into his eyes) Just like on a pitch-black night in a dense forest when a lost traveller, amid the tangled trees, sees a star that guides the way, you are that star for me. The only difference is that the lost traveller's star is in the sky, and my star is right here on earth with me.

After hearing Sangeeta's words, Vinay became emotional. He held Sangeeta's hands firmly and turned his face away.

Sangeeta	:	Hey my Mister! You've changed your posture too early. It's been barely a month since our wedding. You were being very strict, so what happened suddenly?
Vinay	:	(Closing his eyes and trying to hide his tears) Sangeeta, you know I'm strict on principles only.
Sangeeta	:	Your demeanour is quite revealing. Your heart is so pure that in no time your emotions well up in your eyes.
Vinay	:	Yes, I am emotional, but the condition is that these emotions should be genuine.
Sangeeta	:	I'm sorry, Vinay. I feel like sacrificing my life on true emotions.
Vinay	:	Life is so important that it doesn't need to be sacrificed on someone, it should be lived in a way that it becomes an example for others.
Sangeeta	:	Together, we'll create a clean world.

	I apologize, Vinay, for hurting your feelings.
Vinay	: Yes, you've hurt my feelings, but I won't forgive you for that. I sentence you to work hard with me to build a new and better world.
Sangeeta	: I accept the sentence. But there's one condition. Promise me that you'll keep guiding me at every difficult turn in life.
Vinay	: No, I don't accept that condition.
Sangeeta	: So, you'll leave me in a tough situation?
Vinay	: Absolutely not.
Sangeeta	: What kind of joke is this, then?
Vinay	: This is not a joke; it's the truth. Women are still in the middle of various affairs. You haven't become entirely empowered, nor are you entirely helpless. One thing that has never made sense to me is why women who take on the form of Durga still belittle themselves. I understand that advice is necessary in times of trouble, but I also know that sometimes, it's not just advice that's needed; it's also assistance. If you consider me more than just an advisor, I'm ready to stand by your side.
Sangeeta	: (Looking into Vinay's eyes) You are a silly guy, a bad guy, but you're also a very good guy. Mine and only mine.
Vinay	: (Holding Sangeeta's hand and looking into her eyes) You are also quite silly and flawed, but you are a very good girl as well. Mine and only mine. So, my

	dear, now let's head towards the office. Lunchtime is already over during our conversation.
Sangeeta :	Alright, let's go, but one day, I'll make sure that you must meet your dad.
Vinay :	Oh my God! We fought the Mahabharata battle all night, and with great efforts, we finally managed to kill one, unfortunately, that too escaped by morning.

Both of them laugh heartily and exit.
The curtain falls.

******

Act-V Scene-I

Time- 6:30 am
Location- A park in Uttam Nagar, Delhi

Jeevan : What's up, Ramesh? You've been absent from the office, the park, and not even answering the phone calls for the past 15-20 days. I heard from the office that you're on a one- month leave. You seem quite weak. Is everything alright? Well, since you're here, let's go for a couple of rounds around the park. Come on.

Ramesh : How can all things be good in life, Jeevan, my brother? What's life without its ups and downs? I am not interested. Today, you alone may go for walking.

Jeevan : Up to 30-35, our body carries us. Somehow, next ten years pass. After 50, some ailment or the other always seems to crop up and things start changing. Then, it feels like we are carrying our body. We keep wandering like living corpses.

Ramesh : Issues arise not only from internal factors but frequently originate externally as well. From my perspective, the majority of challenges stem from outside influences. We toil ceaselessly, often oblivious to the reality that life encompasses more than just our professional responsibilities. Our unwavering dedication to the workplace results in our home life permeating our professional space, with the office becoming a constant presence in our personal lives. Time that should be devoted to our children and family is consumed by work. Consequently, despite giving our all to the office, we find ourselves not truly helping either our home or workplace. We resemble a dog chasing two bones but catching neither. By the time we reach 50, our children are typically in their mid-20s, creating a noticeable generation gap. Time slips away like sand through our fingers, yet our habits and stubborn nature keep us anchored in the same position.

Jeevan : We've already become dogs, working day and night for the boss, but he never becomes ours. By the time we manage to win the boss over, he receives transfer orders. Flattering the boss consumes so much time that the wife gets upset. We are hung in between. Boss couldn't be pleased and wife couldn't be entertained. What a mess it is, life? We the donkey of our office carry it to home also.

Ramesh : We've always been stuck in between -

between the office and home, between children and work, between the secretary and the wife, between the boss and the subordinates. It's pretty dangerous to live a middle-class life. Our entire life runs on instalments - car instalments, home loan instalments, insurance instalments, instalments for expensive purchases for the home, personal loans instalments, and the monthly committee contributions instalments. We take one loan on one side and pay off another on the other side. Is this what life is all about?

Jeevan : It's fortunate that we get free hospital treatment due to this job; otherwise another instalment would be added to these loans.

Ramesh : You know, middle age, much like the middle class, brings its own set of challenges. Our hair is turning grey, yet our moustaches remain dark, leaving us in a state of neither youth nor old age. The daily grind of going to the office persists, but our stamina is lacking, placing us in a state of neither sickness nor perfect health. The pressures at work and the pursuit of promotions have somewhat isolated us, although we still maintain connections with each other. Thus, we find ourselves in a state of neither complete integration into society nor total detachment. Our spouses may not be giving us the attention we desire, and at this stage, crafting a love story appears near-impossible, positioning us as neither purely lovers nor entirely husbands. After work, we engage in social gatherings, enjoy a drink with friends, yet simultaneously deliver lectures to our children about steering clear of such activities, rendering us neither entirely corrupted nor wholly reformed. Essentially, we exist in a state of in-betweenness.

Jeevan : You can't be reformed anymore; what can I say to you? If I say something, you'll accuse me of delivering a sermon. Hey, sir, the bitterness and disappointment you carry around all the time are easy to discover. These are constantly walking beside us. You don't need to go looking for them. Just a small chance will make them mount on your head. But, for positivity, you need to put in considerable efforts as it often remains hidden somewhere.

Ramesh : Honestly, listening to your wisdom is quite enjoyable. But many times, it's also quite challenging to hear your piercing words.

Jeevan : Let me tell you something from my childhood. My father used to work as a labourer in the city, and occasionally, he'd bring grapes for us. My mother would divide them among all the siblings. Since the grapes were brought by a labourer, their quality was modest, a mixture of both sour and sweet. I had a habit of eating the sour grapes first and savouring the sweet ones last, which made the taste linger in my mouth for a long time. Life's calculations are the same. Confront the bitter hardships first.

Ramesh : Friend, the uniqueness of life is that everyone's problems and their solutions may appear the same, but actually they are different. There is another aspect to this story beyond your story. Grapes were brought by my labourer father also, and I also used to eat sour grapes at first. But as soon as I was left with sweet grapes in my portion, one of my siblings would suddenly snatch them away. I would start crying, and after some mediation by my mother, they would give me the same amount of grapes, but the pity was that they would already have eaten their sweet grapes and only sour grapes of both theirs and mine would remain in my share. These incidents gradually filled my personality with jealousy, hatred, selfishness, greed, and immodesty. I still wander in the attempt to steal someone else's sweet grapes.

Jeevan : Values, my friend, don't collapse in a day. The building of ideals which was built in decades is not destroyed in a day either. After getting a job, we lived the same kind of life for 10-15 years. Those who had come into the job with enthusiasm and honesty began to get hurt every day. The dishonest and lazy ones started receiving rewards. Slowly, when they started to dominate, the walls of ideals and values began to quiver. By the time we touched middle age the building of ideals and values turned into ruins. You are right. Now we are sitting in between, under the open sky. We can't go into this ruin, nor can we completely turn it into a castle of corruption.

Ramesh : We are helpless. Conscience doesn't allow us to become completely corrupt, and the system doesn't let us work with honesty. We are stuck in between. The goal has moved away, and mirages have appeared. The more we advance, the further it moves away. The seed of immorality has been sown on the barren land of values. Now we are reaping the fruits of hybrid trees, eating them ourselves and forcing our children to eat them as well. After this, what hope can we have from the next generation?

Jeevan : Just keep holding on to hope, my friend. All streams of success emerge out of this melting iceberg of optimism. Our values may have suffered some loss, but

	the roots of our culture run so deep that no immorality can cut through them.
Ramesh	: Then, having hidden under the armour of knowledge, let's stop looking at our corrupt surroundings. Danger doesn't spare us if, having seen it approaching, we close our eyes.
Jeevan	: It's not about closing your eyes but keeping them open. Instead of hiding ourselves under the armour of knowledge, we need to wrap it around. This is the shield, my friend, that saves us from all evils. The middle state that you are talking about is the originator of the path of knowledge that offers solution to all problems.
Ramesh	: Listen friend, I am already disturbed. Now, please don't twist your words and confuse me further. Be straightforward in whatever you want to say.
Jeevan	: What I'm trying to convey is that our cultural heritage, deeply rooted in our scriptures, offers us guidance when we find ourselves caught between ethical and unethical choices, essentially serving as a guiding light during the years between 40 and 50. Are you aware that Arjuna, the recipient of wisdom from Sri Krishna through the Bhagavad Gita, was positioned between the two mightiest armies in the world? Similarly, the *Setu* used by Lord Rama and his army to reach Lanka was

constructed right in the middle of two shores. Even formidable warriors like Bhishma, who possessed the blessing of controlling the timing of his death, met his demise due to a person with neuter gender. Strategies to navigate through life's challenges are honed when we find ourselves in amidst the ocean of adversity. Therefore, my friend, it's important to recognize and value this intermediary position.

Ramesh : Now don't turn me into a mule by weaving a web of words. Let me remain either a horse or a donkey.

Jeevan : Don't worry, you'll remain a donkey only. If you've been a donkey all your life, why are you trying to become a horse now? Just remain a donkey.

Ramesh : You're absolutely right, my friend. Until now, we've shouldered everyone else's burdens, but when our own children start weighing on us, we object saying that we are not donkeys.

Jeevan : What happened? Have you had a dispute with your children?

Ramesh : You may consider it true. To preserve what name and respect one has earned until the age of fifty, sometimes you have to go to any extent.

Jeevan : Well, let me tell you something, Ramesh. You're quite a slavish piece, a real hot-tempered fellow. Too much anger isn't a good thing. I remember how you used to beat up your wife for no reason. You've unleashed the anger of your boss on your family members. I have an account of all your atrocities. Poor Manju *Bhabhi* has endured your terror a lot.

Ramesh : Cheap, what medals have you earned by being a slave to your wife? To support your family, run a household, do you know how many hardships one has to bear? I've spent my entire life saving every penny to build my home, educate my children, and make them capable. I may have suffered many hardships, but I made them successful.

Jeevan : Indeed, neither you nor I gained anything. But yes, don't boast of your sacrifices. You are not the only person who has done all of this. You have done nothing to please them. This was your responsibility and your pride which made you do everything. By doing so, you've earned honour more than contentment because your happiness wasn't in your satisfaction but in your prestige. As for the generational gap, this issue plagues everyone, whether they are decent or infuriated. If someone's son is fine, the daughter isn't, and vice versa. And by some coincidence, if both are fine, we ourselves turn problematic. Beyond fifty, problems start coming one after another. Anyway, to be honest, don't take it as an offense, we're not exactly saints, are we?

Ramesh : Hey, you offspring of a philosopher, you've always been a chatterbox. You've always delivered speeches. I live by my principles. But rogues like you don't even know whether one has to provide support to a person in pain or to scratch his wounds with the sharp edged words.

Jeevan : Support! You can take it too, brother. When two destitute people come together, they become each other's support. We've been living in a rented house for a month now. Come join us there.

Ramesh : What? Are you living separately now? You used to act all righteous. Now I understand your mischievous side. After pretending for so long, you are finally exposed. You're a player too, my friend, a big player.

Jeevan : You're absolutely correct, my friend. We all see ourselves as participants in the game of life. We view ourselves as such accomplished champions that we're determined to remain in the game until the emerging generation of remarkable individuals eventually supersedes us. The key message is that those who fail to bridge the generation gap are the ones causing problems. And, my friend, we've also become a part of that group causing such disruptions.

Ramesh : So, did you also have a fight with your

		son? He just got married; you should've let him live his life peacefully at least for a few days. Your son is decent too.
Jeevan	:	My son is decent, but the daughter-in-law is quite a forward girl. She's ultra-modern. I just said one thing that day, 'Wear your clothes properly.' but, on spot, that queen delivered a sermon. A month has passed since she preached. We couldn't bridge the generation gap, but we could separate ourselves from our ego. That's what we did. Kunal rightly says that we also go to the office. Nowadays, in our office also, kids from this generation wear clothes like that. The only difference is that kids of others look good in those clothes, and ours don't.
Ramesh	:	I accept it. We do have double standard. I prefer SpiceJet more than Air India because they have young air hostesses in skimpy foreign outfits. They smile and say 'Hi' two or three times during the entire flight. But tell me, have you accepted that what's happening should happen?
Jeevan	:	You gave your all until circumstances forced a pause. Did you succeed in altering the course of destiny? A clever crow ends up consuming more filth by constantly pecking at it. A wise individual should promptly embrace change by comprehending the nuances of time's workings.

Ramesh : Are you planning to transform into an elderly sage assassin, well beyond the age of 50? You'll be attacking your prey under the pretence of meditation.

Jeevan : Many times, small things teach us big lessons. In our office, we also observe our colleagues, don't we? After all, who is considered old at 50? We keep staring at them with good or bad intentions. And, if we were the bosses, there would be no boundary for us; our debauchery would be well established. Let go of all this fuss. Remember the higher power and spend your time contentedly. By the way, whether you agree or not, we're no saint either.

Ramesh : (Looking at Jeevan angrily) Please refrain from repeating this statement. We've dedicated our entire lives to maintaining our homes, suppressing our own joy, sacrificing our youth, educating our children, and securing employment. What more can we offer? Should we relinquish our lives? You may not be a righteous person, but I believe I am. If the generation gap is indeed significant, why have we followed these esteemed individuals up to this point? Why are we in pursuit of our glorious history? Why do we uphold our traditions? Do you understand why? Because the reality is that we can't gain knowledge from the future, and the present offers us little beyond a fleeting moment. To acquire knowledge, the present must connect with the past. My predecessors, my parents, and my educators are all integral parts of my esteemed history that consistently imparts wisdom. When the upcoming generation, which deems its older generation as foolish, reaches our stage, they will recall their past as they, too, are deemed foolish by their subsequent generation.

Jeevan : By that time, my friend, a full-fledged generation will have come and gone. You'll have observed the erosion of knowledge, the pollution in traditions, the deterioration of values, and humanity being traded openly in the market. In such circumstances, wanderers like us, having lost nearly everything, will only be seeking a brief respite for a couple of moments.

Ramesh : No matter how much philosophy you preach, it won't affect me. I am unwavering in my principles.

Jeevan : How much will you criticize the changes in time, my brother? Don't forget that what we have today is the result of new thinking. All the scientific discoveries, medicines, and conveniences you're enjoying have been brought by those who had innovative thinking. Today, their work is applauded. Nobody cares if they made these discoveries while wearing specific attire, whether they married by their choice or their parents'. Do you know how many people are constantly working to maintain each of these conveniences? Those electric bulbs lighting up your home involve thousands of people working continuously behind the scenes. If you want to learn from the past, learn that civilizations begin from scratch, reach their peak, and then decline to start anew. I can't stop this cycle, and neither can you.

Ramesh : Then why haven't we been able to produce any Valmikis, Vedavyas, Buddhas, Mahavirs, Kabirs, Rahims, or sages for centuries? What kind of progress is this, my brother, where the elderly parents are ousted from their homes in the name of personal freedom, their lives are endangered, the honour of mothers and sisters is spoiled, and the truth is strangled? Shame on such progress!

Jeevan : Forget it, my friend, this is an endless debate. We just need to see whether nature aligns with progress and traditions. Otherwise, let's be content with what we have. I don't know much, but one thing I surely know. If you have the courage to listen.

Ramesh	:	You can talk as much as a flock of crows.
Jeevan	:	Damn, we are not saints either.

As soon as Jeevan said this, Ramesh moved his hand towards his shoes. Seeing his intentions clear, Jeevan ran away and behind him Ramesh is running with shoes in his hand.

Ramesh	:	Stop, you scoundrel, as you might end up with broken bones today!
Jeevan	:	See, my friend, you weren't in the mood for taking a round today, but I've made it happen.

The curtain falls.

******

Act-V Scene-II

Time: 6.00 am
Location: Sector 8, Dwarka, New Delhi.

After being evicted from their house, Jeevan and Jyoti are living on rent in a flat in Dwarka, Delhi. Ramesh still lives alone at his Uttam Nagar house. Both work in the same office, so their friendship is also strong and old. Both their wives are also good friends. One day Jyoti remembered Manju and called her.

Jyoti	:	Hello Manju, it's Jyoti speaking. How are you? It's been many days, and you haven't called or talked to me.
Manju	:	Hi Jyoti. It's good to hear from you after a long time. I'm doing fine, Jyoti. I'm constantly worried about Vinay's father. We are four people here, but he's alone in such a big house. Everything must be bitter and biting to him.
Jyoti	:	Worry is always there, but what can we do? Our control over circumstances is limited.
Manju	:	Alright, tell me, how are you and brother Jeevan? It's been so many days since you called.
Jyoti	:	We've shifted to Dwarka, sister. Come over tomorrow morning at 6 in Sector

		8 Park, and then we can have tea at my place.
Manju	:	Alright, let's meet tomorrow morning.

After saying this, both of them hang up. Jyoti and Manju meet at Dwarka Sector 8 Park at the decided time.

Manju	:	(Looking at Jyoti) Oh Jyoti! What's happened to you? Why do you look so weak? I didn't even recognize you. Is everything okay?
Jyoti	:	You've also become quite weak. Doesn't your daughter-in-law take proper care of you? Come, let's chat as we take a walk.
Manju	:	My daughter Sangeeta is a gem. Despite being so wealthy and having a high-profile job, she's down-to-earth. Even with so much work in the office, she takes care of everyone a lot.
Jyoti	:	So, is her mother creating any trouble?
Manju	:	No, she's a humble woman. She's unwell but stays happy with us. However, she says that having food at her daughter's home feels like a disgrace.
Jyoti	:	There doesn't seem to be any doubt about his behaviour still tell me, how's Vinay doing?
Manju	:	He's doing well in his job. Even now, he takes care of his mother as much as he did before marriage.
Jyoti	:	Then, what's your problem? Why are you getting so weak?
Manju	:	There may or may not be a problem. Vinay and his father are not on talking

terms. God knows how much bitterness has developed between them. I've also made several phone calls, but initially, he didn't answer. When he finally did, he scolded me and said that he should be left alone with his issues.

Jyoti : Perfection doesn't exist in life, sister. Even God leaves us with some imperfections. He gave Dasharath a son like Lord Rama, yet he had to die from separation. Even a devoted child Shravan Kumar couldn't save his parents from suffering in the end. We must find contentment in what we have.

Manju : It hurts my heart a lot, sister. I can't see him in any discomfort, no matter what sort of person he is. After all, we've spent such a long life together. A moment's anger should not weigh heavily on the remaining life.

Jyoti : What can we do, sister? Once children grow up and become sensible, women are left in between husbands and children. They're neither entirely wives nor mothers. They get caught in between. If husband argues with the kids, she takes the kid's side, and when the children misbehave with their father, she sides with her husband.

Manju : You're absolutely right, sister. Husbands can get away with as much misbehaviour as they want, but when they start bothering the children, a mother's inner strength awakens. The real issue comes up around the age of 40-50, when children step into their parents' shoes and start taking their mother's sides.

Jyoti : What can we do, sister? Daughters eventually become strangers, and there's always an inevitable separation. It's a burden that comes with being a wife and a mother. If a solution doesn't emerge, women will either die from their husbands' or their children's separation.

Manju : We can't seem to find a solution. When will the scientists who created vaccines for dangerous viruses like Corona make a vaccine for this virus of hatred which spreads everywhere and often divides families in their own homes? Sometimes the segregation is so deep that it draws a boundary within the house itself. The father stays in one room, and the children in another. The poor mother, caught in between, doesn't know whether to go to her children or her husband.

Jyoti : The only solution is a joint family, but that's nearly impossible in today's world. This virus first attacked the strong defence system of a joint family and destroyed it. When grandparents, uncles, and aunts lived together, they used to manage everything.

Manju : This is also a dilemma. We can't decide

what we really want - a joint family or a nuclear family. When difficulties arise, the idea of a joint family appears more appealing, but when we're content, we lean towards the idea of a nuclear family.

Jyoti : These arguments will keep going on. Let's go home now and have some tea. It's been a long time since we sat together.

Jyoti and Manju enter Jyoti's apartment.

Manju : You've changed your home and didn't even tell me. Well, the security here is better, but it's smaller than the previous one.

Jyoti : How can we compare this home with the old one? But still, according to current needs, this is fine. You sit for two minutes; let me make some tea.

Manju : Has the daughter-in-law gone to her parents' house? Jeevan *Bhai Sahab* is also not here. Where are all the family members?

Jyoti : Everyone is enjoying their own world. The daughter-in-law didn't like being with us, so for the happiness of our son and daughter-in-law, we left that home.

Tears gushed out from Jyoti's eyes.

Manju : So that's the reason for your weakness. But where is Jeevan *Bhai Sahab*?

Jyoti : Every morning, he takes his bike and goes to that park in Uttam Nagar where we used to go for walks. He has a group

	of friends, and Ramesh Bhai Sahab also meets him often. Occasionally, our son also comes. Having talked with his son for a while, he feels happy.
Manju	: Good. But sometimes, you should also go. Meeting everyone will lighten your heart.
Jyoti	: (Wiping her tears) No, sister. I went a couple of times, but I could not stop myself from shedding tears. I spoiled the mood of both father and son. After that, I decided never to go again.
Manju	: You are still not happy. The body is here, but the mind is elsewhere. Get out of this situation, sister, or you'll harm yourself. At least, I find some comfort in the fact that the children, by talking to me with love at least twice a day, lighten the heart.
Jyoti	: (Weeping) Each day, I feel myself diminishing internally. There's an emptiness within me, and nowadays, even meals are cooked by Kunal's father. He makes efforts to console me yet my heart continues to cry.
Manju	: Look, sister, if the children aren't bothering you, then, you shouldn't worry either. Kunal is doing his job properly, isn't he?
Jyoti	: I don't know, sister. I've stopped asking anything. His dad was saying that the pregnant daughter-in-law is going to give birth to a child in 10-15 days.

		During that period, we'll spend some time with the children.
Manju	:	Go for sure, sister. The next generation will free us from the past. When the child arrives, our hearts will find solace. Maybe that's the cure for this ailment.
Jyoti	:	How can I go, sister? A child is about to be born, and neither of them has said anything yet. She used to be as she was, but there was no hope for a son to be like that.
Manju	:	If you keep waiting for them to invite you, you'll end up alone. You must fulfil your duties, and leave the rest to God.
Jyoti	:	Don't talk about duties, sister. You know everything. I gave to this house almost everything needed from my side in the past 25 years. Today even that home is not with me. Oh, why doesn't anyone tell them that I have brought this house to this stage by sacrificing both my career and youth? My happy days had just arrived, and then my children started this drama.
Manju	:	Yashoda didn't know that Krishna whom she raised with such pride would one day leave Gokul, Mathura, and settle in a new city Dwarka. Destiny is mighty; who can control it?
Jyoti	:	My case is the opposite one, sister. Here, Yashoda herself has moved to Dwarika after handing over Gokul Dham to

		Krishna. Whom should I blame, myself or my child?
Manju	:	If you yourself have taken the decision to quit, why cry about it? What you did was your duty. Don't mistake it as a debt on someone, or else you'll suffer both mentally and physically.
Jyoti	:	Hypertension, high blood pressure, diabetes, anaemia, and who knows what else have struck me. The doctor has advised that if I don't engage in morning walks, my condition will worsen. At this age, where else can I go? The scriptures describe four stages of life, but I feel they are only meant for men. The transition to the *Vanaprastha* and *Sannyasa* stages aren't for women. For a middle aged woman, going to the forest means losing life.
Manju	:	I agree with that. Even approaching 50, we're not entirely safe from the risks of abduction and rape. Society remains the same, rather worsening. Even today, if it's revealed that we're alone and helpless, our lives will be in danger.
Jyoti	:	It's the same situation of being in between. We can't stay at home nor is it possible to leave it. So, the only option is to slowly kill us right here.
Manju	:	Vanaprastha isn't necessary. Aren't we in a more alarming situation than being in the wilderness? Those we once cared for have turned their backs on us.

Even at our age, potential threats are all around. It's as though the ferocity of wild animals has found its way into human nature. Everywhere you look, there's a lurking danger. It's only the matter of an opportunity for an attack to occur.

Jyoti : A man's recklessness doesn't consider age or relationships. There must be some solution to this problem, or perhaps we're destined to suffer through life's hardships.

Manju : Every problem has a solution. We just need to change our perspective. Age-related diseases have affected even those living with their children. No one is entirely enjoying good physical and mental health. We seek solution of current problems in past. Sangeeta's mother has started to recover. There are two more women in our neighbourhood like us. You should come and join us. We've formed a self-help group with government assistance. If we engage ourselves in some work, it will keep our minds occupied. By helping the needy, we can continue our *Vanaprastha* here, and by remaining detached even while serving, we can achieve our *Sannyasa* right here.

Jyoti : Advice is good, sister, but it might be too late now. Due to high blood pressure and diabetes, there's hardly any strength

		left in my body. Nevertheless, I'll try for a few days.
Manju	:	Alright, sister, take care of yourself. I'm heading off now. I thought I would meet Jivan Bhai Sahab as well, but he hasn't come. I'll visit some another time.

Manju leaves
The curtain falls.

******

Act-V Scene-III

Time- 10 o'clock in the day.
Location- House of Life in Dwarka, Delhi
Manju went home and told the whole story of Jyoti's house to Vinay and Sangeeta. Everyone together made a plan that only Avtar Singh can help in such a situation. So Avtar Singh was called by phone. Jyoti took Sangeeta to her house. Avtar Singh and Ramesh also came to Jeevan's Dwarka flat.

Avtar Singh	:	Well, I don't really have the right to speak on a matter so personal, but if both of you permit, I'd like to say something.
Jeevan	:	You are our guest, and in age, you seem older than we are. You can say whatever you want without hesitation.
Avtar Singh	:	First, let me clarify that I have no bias towards anyone. Sangeeta has called me, but I want to talk impartially.
Ramesh	:	(Upon hearing Sangeeta's name, wrinkles appears on his forehead) So, you're the sympathizer and guardian of that girl?
Avtar Singh	:	Well said, you are right. I am both Sangeeta's sympathizer and protector. She is the daughter of a friend of mine, and she means more to me than a daughter.

Ramesh	:	(Slightly agitated) How can you claim to be impartial? You're playing the tricks of a policeman.
Jeevan	:	Does your anger ever subside, or will it always be like this? He has come here from Jaipur. Let's hear the full story first. (Turning towards Avtar Singh) Please go ahead, Inspector Sahab.
Ramesh	:	But having provided information that she is his friend's daughter and that he is her sympathizer and guardian, he has already drawn a conclusion before discussing. So how can this be in our favour?
Jeevan	:	It seems like stress and illness have mentally and physically weakened you. You've already reached a conclusion without hearing the whole story. (Turns back to Avtar Singh) Please speak, Inspector Sahab.
Avtar Singh	:	Listen to me once, and then you can draw your conclusions and make your decisions. I'll accept whatever you decide.
Ramesh	:	(In a sarcastic tone, with folded hands) You are a policeman, an inspector, and you are also the representative from the girl's side. If we don't listen to you, you might arrest us and put us behind bars. Still, I humbly request you to resolve one of my cases, and then, if you wish, you can put me in jail.
Jeevan	:	Ramesh, what's gotten into you? You're crossing all the boundaries of decency.

		Just think that Inspector Sahab is our guest.
Avtar Singh	:	Let him speak, Jeevan Sahab, I want to hear him first. Please go ahead, Ramesh Ji. How can I assist you?
Ramesh	:	Before you register a case against me, please hear my complaint. A girl not only trapped my well-behaved son with her charms but also married him and separated him from us. What sections of your law are applied against this, and what is the provision of punishment?
Jeevan	:	Your mind has gone astray, Ramesh. How much will you blame that girl? Now it's time to mend your habits. You are also part of the "weakness leads to too much anger" story.
Avtar Singh	:	I request you, Jeevan Sahab, to let him say what he wants to say. Let him allow the internal stifling to dissipate. Let pent-up feelings and thoughts be released that have been concealed for months. How can we find a solution to his problems without hearing him? Yes, Ramesh Ji, please continue.
Ramesh	:	Suffocation is inevitable, Inspector Sahab. If someone takes away your lifelong earnings in a moment and leaves you wandering helpless on the streets, what will you do then?
Avtar Singh	:	Do you want to say more, or should I begin answering your questions?
Ramesh	:	There are countless questions in my

	mind, but first, please answer these questions.
Avtar Singh	: Look, Ramesh Ji, your son married the girl of his choice, and both of them are adults. The law remains silent on this matter because it's their personal choice. However, if someone has separated you from your son, the law advocates taking strict action in such cases. Please tell me in detail what has happened.
Ramesh	: You are a policeman. You're playing with words. You know very well what has happened. Still, for your satisfaction, I will explain everything to you.

Ramesh narrates the whole story in detail.

Avtar Singh	: (After hearing Ramesh's entire story) It's really a very painful story, Ramesh Ji. You've been going through severe mental and physical agony for the past six to seven months. Can you please tell me what kind of girl you wanted for your son?
Ramesh	: Inspector Sahab, you are wise enough to understand it. We work at the Central Secretariat, live in the capital city, and have earned a good reputation so far. So, we expected a match with the same standards. I haven't set up an orphanage or care home where anyone could be brought. I had already discussed a suitable match with one of my colleagues. The girl is a professor right here in Delhi University. But, what can

	I do, Sahab? That girl ensnared my boy into her web. Everything came crashing down, and we were humiliated too.
Avtar Singh	: So, is it just because of this that your son and wife left home?
Ramesh	: No, they didn't just leave home; I threw them out. My wife was supporting our son's stance so she also went with him. Well, brother, problems come into everyone's life. If there had been a problem with that girl, she should have talked to me. I would have contacted the Ministry of Social Justice and Empowerment and got her mother's treatment arranged. I could have also arranged her marriage in a good family. But she chose a shortcut and looted everything from me in no time.
Avtar Singh	: You indeed have a good heart. But one thing I know is that the woman staying with Sangeeta is not her mother. Her mother has passed away long back.
Ramesh	: What? She's not her mother? Then who is she?
Avtar Singh	: She is the elder sister of Sangeeta's mother. As for her family background, she comes from a highly respected family. Her father was an extremely honest police officer. Her mother was very cultured and noble. Money was never an issue for her. Her maternal grandfather also belonged to the

aristocratic class of his time. He had only two daughters, and both were the sole owners of all the property. Her mother passed away and her aunt is with her. Her aunt's husband also passed away. That's why, even before the marriage, she transferred all her property to Sangeeta's name. She is already worth three to four crores. She holds a high position in a multinational company, similar to your son. She gets an annual salary package of 24 lakhs. She is beautiful, well-educated, and elegant. (After telling Ramesh the entire story, Avtar Singh continued) Look at her photo and now tell me, what is lacking in Sangeeta?

Ramesh : (Expanding his eyes) Inspector, what kind of story have you made me listen to? Is what you're saying really true?

Avtar Singh : Yes, it's hundred percent true. In fact, I'd say that your family and your son didn't match Sangeeta. I believe your son must have ensnared Sangeeta after seeing her wealth. Now, tell me, should the police apply appropriate sections on your son for trapping my deceased friend's daughter?

Ramesh : (Holding his head and sitting on the sofa) Oh my God! If it's true, then maybe I've made a huge mistake, Inspector Sahab.

Jeevan : Better late than never; let's make things

		right. At least you've admitted your mistake.
Avtar Singh	:	It's human nature, Jeevan Sahab. When it backfires on them, they admit their mistake; otherwise, they don't miss any chance to disgrace others. False pride and arrogance are like two magical lenses in the glasses of some people through which they see only what they want to see. Everything else is blurred. Ramesh ji, before being so arrogant, you should have taken care of your health. Now go, and before your son and daughter-in-law come to pick you up and embarrass you, go to them yourself and spend the rest of your life in happiness.
Ramesh	:	(To himself feeling remorseful) What have I done? I've poisoned my own family's life. God, please don't forgive me for this sin.
Avtar Singh	:	What are you thinking, Ramesh Ji? Do you doubt my words?
Ramesh	:	No, Inspector, There is no scope left for doubt. I'm thinking that, for the first time in my life, I've believed someone's words so completely. After working at the Central Secretariat, doubting everything has become a habit, so trusting someone at the first instance is almost impossible.
Avtar Singh	:	Sir, it seems like your habit has overtaken even us police officers in doubting.
Ramesh	:	This is exactly what I'm thinking.

	Even you police officers are masters in suspicion. Your work starts with suspicion.
Avtar Singh	: Well then, get up, go to your children, and give them the benefit of your love.
Ramesh	: No, Inspector Sahab, how can I face them now? Vinay and Manju, it's alright, but how can I face that girl, whom I've wronged? Who knows what I've said about her.
Avtar Singh	: Then, will you remain distant from the roots? Go ahead, and see, Sangeeta is eagerly waiting to welcome you warmly.
Ramesh	: It's not feasible to detach oneself from their origins, Inspector Sahab. However, as a tree grows large and substantial, proper roots appear to provide support and sustenance. At that point, the presence or absence of the original roots hardly matter.
Jeevan	: You are absolutely right. The roots affected by termites can't support the tree. Such roots should be cut and thrown away.
Ramesh	: (Slightly gloomy, resting his hand on Jeevan's shoulder) You're right, my friend. Do me a favor, Jeevan. Put an end to my life. Go to the kitchen, get a knife, and cut me into pieces.
Avtar Singh	: Realizing one's mistake is also a great thing. Don't feel so bad, it's not your fault.

Ramesh	:	It's a grave fault, Inspector Sahab. I should receive a punishment in equal proportion.
Avtar Singh	:	Individuals are essentially guided by the passage of time. In the current era, both you and I find ourselves in a transitional phase. We aim to instill independence in our children today, yet we hesitate to allow them full autonomy in decision-making. We hope for their wisdom but not to surpass our own. We desire their obedience, but solely directed towards us. While we aim to grant them ownership of property, land, or responsibilities, we simultaneously wish to maintain control over them as if they were subservient to us. Reflect upon the conflicting conduct we are embracing. What kind of model of humanity do we embody by following this contradictory path? Even then we need a true son. We show gratitude of being elder and win sympathy as well. Oh God! What a specimen called human you have designed?
Jeevan	:	Besides this, we have one more illness, Thanedar Sahab. If sons-in-law and daughter- in-law are of my choice and belong to my caste, they are noble otherwise they are inferior. In Indian culture, the tradition of choosing a partner was not prevalent among grooms but rested on the girl. She

	used to choose her life partner, and the entire family and society accepted her decision.
Avtar Singh	: Every age has its own cultural values and traditions, Jeevan Sahab. In the age you are talking about, children were made so capable that there was no doubt about their decision making power.
Jeevan	: But Inspector Sahab, if they adopt those values, that culture, those traditions today, what's wrong with it?
Avtar Singh	: Every age has its own properties. The benchmarks of life values are different. Ways of living are different. Deceiving plays a significant role in the current era. Being in the police, I have come to realize that the bigger the deceiver, the more successful they are. The best example of this is politics. In the past 70 years, we have made our country and its citizens utter fools. When there is an abundance of fear, deception, trickery, and injustice all around, it is natural for parents to be apprehensive about their children.
Jeevan	: Does that mean Ramesh hasn't make a mistake?
Avtar Singh	: He did make a mistake. He was continually searching for a girl who would bring dowry greater than their status or even more. Regardless of what they say, the boy's parents cleverly select a girl from such a family who brings a

	hefty dowry without asking. He should have met with Sangeeta before making any decision.
Jeevan	: This stubbornness has always been there in him. Anger is there too. Most decisions made in anger are wrong. Am I right, Ramesh? (Jeevan looks back when Ramesh doesn't respond) Where did he go? He left without saying anything. You see, Inspector Sahab, he won't change.
Avtar Singh	: Time improves even the worst of people, Jeevan Sahab. Let them go. Today, they have realized their mistake. They will make amends and return to their families.
Jeevan	: Today, you have shown us the reality, Lord. I have never seen a policeman with such pure thoughts before.
Avtar Singh	: Policemen, like anyone else, are human beings. The influence of power and greed has led them to the way of corruption. When a just leader emerges, they will undergo swift reform.
Jeevan	: Let's go, Lord! Now, please enjoy a cup of tea from my hands. I am coming back from the kitchen with a cup of tea.

Jeevan exits.
The Curtain falls.

******

Act-V Scene-IV

Time: 5 AM.
Location : On the Banks of Ganga in Haridwar.
The next day, Jeevan and Ramesh take leave for a week and come to Haridwar. Both of them are sitting on the sand on the banks of the Ganga, away from the hustle and bustle of the city.

Jeevan	:	How much repentance will you feel? Let go of the past and start anew. Life beckons to you. Don't let this opportunity slip away.

Ramesh remains silent for a minute.

Jeevan	:	Why don't you speak now? Sitting by Ganga Maa in the morning, are you going to observe silence?
Ramesh	:	(After a short silence) Jeevan Bhai, do you know why I have come here?
Jeevan	:	For nothing, you have come just to bake me up? Everyone has troubled me; you can also bring me woes.
Ramesh	:	You've grasped it quite accurately. Truly, this was my plan all along. However, it's not only you; I've come here to transform myself as well. We've both reached the age of 50, our hair has turned grey, but our minds are still inexperienced.

Jeevan	:	Couldn't you do this work elsewhere? Why did you bring me here?
Ramesh	:	(Getting up) Come with me. I'll take you somewhere else.
Jeevan	:	(Getting up and walking with Ramesh) But where?
Ramesh	:	(Pointing towards an ashram) To that ashram. Before coming here, my section officer told me that if we have time, we should visit Kalyan Nath Ashram at least once. I'm taking you there only. I've heard that the disciple of Saint Kalyan Nath, Shri Sadashiv Nath Ji, is 95 years old and very knowledgeable, and he is still in good health. Maybe you'll find solutions to all your problems there.

A little later, Ramesh and Jeevan enter the Kalyan Nath Ashram.

Ramesh	:	Adesh Nath Ji! If you permit, we'd like to sit with you and have the benefit of discussion.
Sadashiv Nath	:	May Lord Shiva's blessings be upon you. Have you come from Delhi?
Ramesh	:	Yes, Prabhu. We have come from Delhi.
Sadashiv Nath	:	Please, have a seat. Even before your arrival, one of my well-wishers informed me about it.
Ramesh	:	Thank you, Maharaj. We have come under your shelter with a desire to acquire some knowledge. Please bestow your grace upon us.
Sadashiv Nath	:	Tell me, what is your problem?
Ramesh	:	Baba, there is a problem, but also not so grave. This mundane life and problems

	often go hand in hand. I have come here to avoid those problems for a few days. But my friend has no idea what's special about this place.
Sadashiv Nath :	Listen, devotee, this is a sacred land. Even the wisest of sages and seers acknowledge its significance. If someone seeks clothes in a gold shop or vice-versa, it is a mismatch of purpose. Fire's inherent nature is to burn, regardless of whether someone steps on it deliberately or accidentally. Yet, the remarkable aspect of that very fire is that when used in the right measure, it also serves to cook. Similarly, this hallowed land is renowned for its abundance of positive energy. So, there's no need to doubt your choice in coming here.
Jeevan :	That wasn't my point, Maharaj. I was eager to know what qualities this land holds.
Sadashiv Nath :	Child, ask what isn't here in this land? Here, there are principles, art, effort, knowledge, vision, culture, education, wealth, yoga, happiness, contentment, and the path to liberation.
Jeevan :	Yes, Mahatma Ji, that's undoubtedly true. After coming here, a state of uncertainty becomes decisive in just a few moments. But my friend is not able to make a decision.
Sadashiv Nath :	What's the dilemma?
Jeevan :	Well, some time ago, he had conflicts

	with his family, and after that, he started living separately in a different place and his family at another place. Now, his family is requesting him to live together, but he is not willing to accept it.
Sadashiv Nath :	As you see this flowing water, my dear, it serves as a symbol of the passage of time. Once it has moved on, it can't be retrieved. It's possible that the opportunities for living together with his family have slipped away with time. Pondering their return might be in vain.
Jeevan :	I have got it, Baba. There wouldn't have been a conflict in my home if I had understood this uniqueness earlier. No two persons can think alike. The Mahabharata happened over the episode of Draupadi's disrobing, and an argument in my home escalated over wearing decent clothes.
Sadashiv Nath :	The issue of clothing is merely a pretext. Dissension was inevitable. Consider the two banks of the Ganges, my child. These banks persist as long as there is water between them. Once the water recedes, neither the river, nor the banks, nor any relationships endure. Similarly, between relationships, a river of love and trust flows. When this river runs dry, there's nothing left. It's important to understand that this river neither starts flowing nor dries up overnight. Just as the fruit on a tree doesn't

		appear or vanish in a day, likewise, the culmination of any action is well-prepared in advance.
Jeevan	:	But some people are being punished for no reason at all.
Sadashiv Nath	:	Your viewpoint is subjective. It's quite improbable that someone would face unfair punishment without a reason. If everyone comprehends the principle of cause and effect, life would be less complicated. If your daughter-in-law refuses to have you stay in your own home, there must be a rationale behind it. It's conceivable that one party has fewer mistakes, while the other possesses more. I mentioned earlier that to reveal itself, sometimes the cause may cross the boundaries of life multiple times. Time isn't confined by the onset and conclusion of our lives. No one can predict when and what will transpire.
Ramesh	:	(Thinking to himself) Oh God! Baba has shifted from discreet embarrassment to open shame. (Changing the subject) But, Baba, there must be some solution to these problems eventually.
Sadashiv Nath	:	Everyone says that humans are great artists. But in reality, they lack artistry. That's why they believe in destruction rather than creation. True art is a means of salvation. It is said that a person who is deprived of literature, music, and art is like an animal without a tail and horns.

Ramesh : Yes, Maharaj, you are absolutely right. Now, we should make an effort to leave our destructive artistry behind.

Sadashiv Nath : This is only possible when we receive the grace of the Supreme Being. Righteousness, unrighteousness, detachment, attachment, wealth, poverty, knowledge, ignorance – all of these are factors leading to bondage. Whether you make a resolution to live with your family or separately, you will still be bound to the concept of family.

Jeevan : But Baba, I've always heard and read that knowledge opens the door to liberation. So, how can knowledge be the cause of bondage?

Sadashiv Nath : You've heard correctly, my child. Knowledge indeed grants liberation. However, who will determine what the definition of true knowledge is? In the age we live in, the arrogance of knowledge has a place higher than knowledge itself. Yes, of course, knowledge may help one understand the causes of bondage. How can it be a cause of bondage?

Jeevan : But scriptures say that knowledge is like fire that burns away impurities.

Sadashiv Nath : What's written in books may or may not be true knowledge. In every era, scriptures are interpreted to suit the needs of that time. The knowledge

	contained in them may be true for that era, but it's not an eternal truth.
Jeevan	: So, are the books misleading, Maharaj?
Sadashiv Nath	: Knowledge arises as a result of the right experiences at the right time and with the right mind-set. Man's mind is the storehouse of knowledge, greater than any book. Our minds should be pure because our mental patterns have been following us from one lifetime to the next, agitating the calmness of our consciousness. When this mind becomes tranquil, the true image reveals itself.
Ramesh	: Baba, have some mercy on us too. I've been saying for a while now that we're past fifty, and this stage is about tranquillity, not getting entangled in desires anymore.
Sadashiv Nath	: Knowledge is akin to a mute person tasting jaggery, my dear. While he has savored it, experienced it, he remains unable to articulate the flavor. In this land, there has consistently existed a distinctiveness – knowledge can manifest unexpectedly at any moment. It may be found drifting with the breeze, having respite on tree branches, meandering along with rivers, roaming through the forests, gracefully dancing on mountain peaks, crackling within flames, soaring among the clouds, and every now and then, it even manages to flourish in the most unlikely

	circumstances. I have never observed my Guruji attending any Gurukul or delving into any scriptures. Yet, from the pristine flow of Mother Ganga right beside this ashram, no one knows when he purified his inner self. He became so illuminated that, even after his transition to the next realm, the radiance of his wisdom continues to shower upon us.
Jeevan :	We consider ourselves very lucky to have met you and received the valuable insights you've shared. You're absolutely correct; fire burns, whether someone approached it consciously or not. Baba, today, we feel a profound sense of gratitude because we've managed to cook our own two pieces of bread in the intense fire of wisdom that resides within you. So, kindly guide us on our next steps.
Sadashiv Nath :	Vats, await the grace of Lord Shiva. After all, who is Baba to orchestrate events for anyone? Life should be naturally unfolded, much like the rhythmic flow of breath. A person's abilities don't govern the grand design of the Creator. The primary objective should be to carry out one's preordained deeds. Go, sit by the banks of Mother Ganga tomorrow morning with a calm mind, and listen to the voice within. Do exactly as suggested. Don't forget to empty your mind before sitting. If even a single

memory lingers, the mind will only express what's left in it. Empty it, if only for a while. Knowledge will manifest itself in that emptiness and then, your path will start to become clear.

With respect, Jeevan and Ramesh take their leave.
The curtain falls.

****

Act-V Scene-V

Time- 11 am.
Location- Arogya Jyoti Hospital in Dwarka, Delhi.

Ramesh and Jeevan have not met for six-seven months. One day, due to a sudden heart attack, Jeevan was admitted to the Intensive Care Unit of Arogya Jyoti Hospital in Dwarka, New Delhi. There, it was found that Ramesh was paralyzed and he had been admitted there for 15 days already. When both of them recovered a little after fighting their respective diseases, they were shifted to the general ward. The beds of both the patients are side by side. Jeevan, seeing Ramesh, comes to meet him. Both of them come alive from the clutches of death. Hence, there was a complete transformation in both of them.

Jeevan : (Having looked at Ramesh with teary eyes) I did tell you to stay calm, but it seems you scoundrel rarely listen. Your anger and emotions have taken a heavy toll, haven't they?

Ramesh : (Struggling to speak clearly as he's had a paralysis stroke on the right side, his hand, leg, and jaw aren't working properly, but he's making an effort to speak) You rogue! Did you even follow my advice? I know you've had a heart attack. You didn't even inform Jyoti Bhabhi and your son.

Jeevan : (Looking away gloomily and muttering

	to himself) How would he know that Jyoti is no more? I can't explain it even if I want to. It's been six months, and I still haven't told him.
Ramesh	: I can't speak loudly. If you don't want to call her now, that's fine. But don't turn away from me. You're the only one I can talk to properly. Well, tell me, how Jyoti Bhabhi is doing. Have you two had a fight too? The two of you are a perfect example of an ideal couple. Don't torment her anymore; go ahead and call her.
Jeevan	: (Having turned his face towards Ramesh) I didn't have a fight with her; that fool had had a fight with her fate. Perhaps her angry destiny snatched away her life.
Ramesh	: What nonsense is this? Has Jyoti sister-in-law passed away? But how?
Jeevan	: She used to curse God every day, questioning the reason for the heavy punishment we seemed to endure. Every day, she pleaded for her life to end. Perhaps one day, her prayers were answered, and God released her. She experienced a severe heart attack, and within five minutes, the light of her existence faded away. It has been half a year since she departed, and I'm uncertain about the purpose of carrying this physical shell when my soul is no more. That's why I haven't shared this with Kunal either.

Ramesh : Why haven't you died yet, O wretched man? Hey, God! What was her fault? She spent her entire life honestly fulfilling her duties, and when the day to live a comfortable life arrived, you couldn't see her enjoying good time. Scoundrel, you are not *Jeevan* (life) you are Mrityu (death), only Mrity. My lovely sister-in-law has departed, and you didn't even inform me. Am I such a big sinner that I couldn't even offer a stick in her pyre?

Jeevan : You're not the sinner, my friend, rather I am the one. Maybe that's why I haven't been liberated yet. I might still have to endure punishment for my sins.

Ramesh : You'll be cast into hell for sure. Don't talk to me after today. I don't even want to see the face of a wretched person like you.

Jeevan : (Displaying both sadness and a smile on his face) Alright, I won't talk to you after today, but today is allowed, isn't it? You haven't spoken to me in the past six months either. I phoned you a couple of times, but you didn't respond.

Ramesh : If I didn't answer your phone, you could have come home. My office is only a five- minute drive from yours.

Jeevan : I tried calling, but you didn't pick up. Jyoti's death was such a terrible blow that I couldn't even get out of bed for a month. Well, leave me alone and think about your wife. She's still alive, after all. Why don't you call her? Enough of this drama. Give me your son's contact; I'll call him now.

Ramesh : (While waving his hand) No, Jeevan Bhai, it was you who emphasized that we must bear the consequences of our actions. This is the repercussion of my deeds, and there's no reason for someone else to bear the blame. I'm currently receiving my salary, and in the future, I'll be entitled to a substantial pension that will ensure my comfortable well-being. Recall our visit to Haridwar when Sadashiv Nath Ji Maharaj advised us to heed the inner voice? I've listened to my inner voice and have devised a plan for the future accordingly. You'll learn about it in a day or two. At this stage of life, with our hair turned grey, our physical strength waning, and the future appearing uncertain, it's not fair to transfer our pain onto others.

Jeevan : Alright, let's do one thing. Both of us should inform our children. I believe they'll rush over when they hear it. Sangeeta and Vinay will definitely come, and I think Kunal still has some decency left in him.

Ramesh : No, Jeevan brother. It's also our duty to give value to our values. If we leave our values aside, how long can we keep blackmailing our children in the name of values. Now is the time to atone for our sins. So, we'll do that.

Jeevan : Why do you always take the blame on yourself? No matter how much philosophy I might preach, the present generation is even worse than us. In my childhood in the village, if someone died young, we were told that the person died but his soul was wandering. But when you look at today's generation, their lack of empathy makes you think that their souls have gone and their bodies are just wandering. In fact, we are living among the dead.

Ramesh : As you sow, so shall you reap. The next generation hasn't fallen from the sky. They are our legacy. The father is rude, arrogant, and debauched and expects his son to be obedient and caring like Shravan Kumar. How can you expect anything else from them?

Jeevan : And what about those whose fathers are perfectly fine? They turn out to be worth nothing.

Ramesh : Go back to the past. Learn something. *Kansas* to *Aggrasens,* and *Prahladas* to *Hiranyakashyaps* have been taking birth since ages. There is nothing new here. No matter how fertile the soil is and how well the seeds are sown, if there are many weeds then the plant will never grow well. It's not just about teaching values; it's about living by example. In our kids' childhood, we were caught up in the intoxication of youth. Now that we are middle-aged, our children are under the effect of the same intoxication, even a bit more. What kind of relationships and what dignity we can expect from the intoxicated ones? I don't know whether I should cry for my follies or for theirs. We've been given a chance; let's try to bridge the gap between the two generations. What we want, we should first become ourselves. Let the days wasted in vain be spent on cleaning up, first inside, then outside. Why are you thinking about getting tangled up in the household at this juncture? We'll put together all our savings and open an Old Age Home and a primary school. If we take good care of the young plants from the beginning, they'll bear good fruit in the future.

Jeevan : I've taken care of my children all my life. What sweet fruit have I received in return? Despite having everything, today, we find ourselves helpless in a hospital bed.

Ramesh : Do you know our major shortcoming? We perceive the responsibility of caring for our family as a kindness, and over time, this duty transforms into a sense of superiority. We begin to convince ourselves that we solely are responsible for the entire family. Eventually, we assume the role of masters, while the rest of the family is relegated to the status of servants. This is when the proverb proves true: 'As one believes, so he becomes.'

Jeevan : (looking in astonishment at Ramesh) "Oh my God! Have you had a stroke, or has the divine performed surgery of your heart and mind? Your sixth sense seems to have awakened. You've become a true sage. Hail Baba Rameshwardas Maharaj! May the Lord bestow His blessings upon this devotee as well!

Ramesh : Well, let me share one last piece of wisdom with you. I hope you won't take it otherwise.

Jeevan : Please, go ahead, my Lord. All is well if it ends well.

Ramesh : Well, we are not saints either.

Upon hearing his dialogue from Ramesh, Jeevan's eyes wells up. He hugs Ramesh sobbing. Suddenly, while shedding tears, some hazy images emerge before his eyes moving toward the door of his room and his bed as well.

Jeevan : (Wiping his tears out) Just turn around, my brother, and see who have come to see you.

Ramesh : (Turning his head) You people? Why did you have to endure the trouble? You could wait for a few days. I will be discharged in a couple of days. (Gesturing towards Jeevan) This scoundrel must have troubled you.

Manju : (With teary eyes) How much more punishment will you give us and

	yourselves too? You could have at least informed us.
Ramesh	: (Raising left hand's finger) Why should you suffer the consequences of my mistakes? Let me atone for it. Don't you remember how I got you all out, pushing and shoving? Now, my ego, like a knife, has stabbed my own heart deeply.
Manju	: It was but me who lost my sense that day. Forget seven lifetimes; I couldn't even fulfil my promise for this birth alone.
Ramesh	: All this is unfair. Such customs are the means of torture carried out to keep women oppressed and silent. Why doesn't a man fulfil the promise of seven lifetimes? You were not at fault that day.
Sangeeta	: (Speaking between the two) It's all my fault, Papa. I can't forgive myself for the rest of my life.
Ramesh	: (Waving finger of his hand) I'm the sinner, my child. I couldn't even bless my beautiful, virtuous daughter-in-law. What could be a greater punishment for me? Come here. I want to place my disabled hand of blessing on your head. Come, my child, take the blessing of your wicked father-in-law.
Sangeeta	: (Placing Ramesh's hand on her head and crying) I have been yearning for this blessing for so many days. I never imagined that the God would grant me this gift in such a condition. (*Wiping her*

	tears) Don't worry, Papa. I have been in touch with the best doctors in the city, and they will start your treatment tomorrow. Both of you will recover soon.
Jeevan	: (Looking at Sangeeta) My Child, may God bless everyone with a daughter-in-law like you. But it seems now that our treatment is in the hands of a supreme power. This isn't something any doctor can handle.
Sangeeta	: I am grateful to you, uncle. If you hadn't informed us, we wouldn't have even known.
Ramesh	: (Glancing at Jeevan) This scoundrel was asking for your contacts, and he called even before I could give him. You will go to hell. You… good-for-nothing.
Jeevan	: No worries, brother. I believe that the hell you are blessing me with must be better than this hell. And yes, you will be there to talk to me.
Kunal	: (Hastening over to his father and hugging him while crying) You're right, Dad. We've turned your life into something worse than the hell. But not anymore. For that, if I have to leave Anju, I will do that. I've lost everything. My Mom passed away due to my wrong decision, and now my dad is in such a bad condition. What's the point of such a life where my parents suffer?

Jeevan	:	Don't blame yourself, son. Perhaps this was my destiny.
Ramesh	:	Kunal, my son, can I ask you something?
Kunal	:	Of course, Uncle. Please ask.
Ramesh	:	My nature has always been fierce. I've tortured my children a lot, snatched away my wife's rights. That's why I'm in this state now. But Jeevan has been a very concerned father. Why are you punishing him, my boy? A father like him is hard to find.
Kunal	:	You're right, uncle. This is all due to my silence. In the name of modernity and privacy, we can't harm our parents. If Anju has a problem, she can live separately. I can't risk my parents' lives for her privacy and false prestige.
Jeevan	:	(Looking at Ramesh with an artificially angry expression) Why are you unnecessarily provoking my child? Just let him live a peaceful life.
Ramesh	:	You have provoked my family, but now that it's your turn, you're feeling the heat.
Manju	:	(Addressing Jeevan) No one is provoking anyone, Bhai Sahab. I'm well aware that you and sister Jyoti are very straightforward and simple. Even Kunal is admitting to that. Anju shouldn't have caused trouble for you all.
Ramesh	:	Her analysis is far better than mine. Now, if she's saying that there was an

injustice with you, it definitely means, it was there.

Kunal : Aunt is absolutely right, Dad. You've been unjustly treated, but I won't allow it anymore.

Jeevan : No, son, I don't want to cause trouble for you all for my own selfishness. Jyoti has already left, and I only have a few days left as well. If you and Anju live peacefully in our absence, it's not a problem.

Ramesh : My friend is absolutely right, son. Our paths won't be intertwined with yours anymore. We've both decided to take VRS (Voluntary Retirement form Service) and live the rest of our lives on our own terms.

Sangeeta : Alright, Dad, we won't come in between both of you, but you can still allow us to help you live your life your way.

Ramesh : (Looking at Jeevan) Perhaps it won't be needed because I've appointed a Deputy Secretary from the Indian Government to take care of me. I've become disabled, my face is twisted and one hand barely functions. In this condition, someone needs to take care of me.

Jeevan : Your limbs and speech have twisted after you had stroke but your mind was already crooked. Just listen to what your daughter-in-law says. I'll be at your service. I have to bear the consequences of deeds, both mine and yours.

Ramesh	:	If you want to live with your family, you can go. I'm not forcing you, but I have already made up my mind, and my decision is firm. I've already caused a lot of trouble for my family. That's enough. (Turning towards Sangeeta) My child, there has developed a strong desire to feel grateful after eating a meal prepared by such a cultured daughter-in-law like you, but now my desires are pacified by my determination.
Sangeeta	:	What kind of resolution have you made which doesn't accept our role even as a servant?
Ramesh	:	Well, child, if you are so adamant, let me tell you that I have resolved to make children cultured.
Jeevan	:	(Surprised) Resolution to make children cultured, hmmm. But how?
Ramesh	:	Jeevan Bhai, since the day Inspector Avtar Singh told us the reality about Sangeeta, I was filled with so much guilt that I wanted to do something good for the rest of my life. So, I sold my ancestral property and bought a thousand-square-yard land in Haridwar. The construction work for its boundaries is underway. My plan is to establish an institution there which may focus on Indian knowledge tradition, science, and education having cultural values. But I didn't know that nature would cripple me. Nevertheless, my

spirit remains undaunted, even though my body is deformed. Right now, I have some budget constraints. I will invest the VRS (Voluntary Retirement from Services) money into it.

Jeevan : You have fulfilled my soul's desires. Jyoti and I used to dream of doing something like this. Now, I'm ready to serve you.

Sangeeta : Papa, we have no objections to your initiative. But I wish that all of us could contribute to this noble cause. I own a significant amount of property of my parents and my aunt in my name. My mother had a strong desire to put her property to good use. If you permit, we'd like to help you implement your plan more effectively.

Jeevan : (Seeing Ramesh deep in thought) What's on your mind? Listen to your daughter-in- law. If she wishes it, then agree to her proposal. It's great that our son and daughter-in-law have achieved financial independence. They now want to support us instead of being dependent on us. Don't hesitate to do a good thing. Just give your approval.

Ramesh : But Jeevan, why should we deplete their savings?

Sangeeta : Papa, no one's wealth really belongs to anyone. I don't even feel like spending on the money I got from my aunt and mom on myself. God has given us so

		much that we don't even feel the need. I want that money to be used for good causes.
Ramesh	:	My child, I cannot use the money of those I have abused. Whatever money Jeevan and I have earned together will be enough for the purpose. I have left selfishness and greed behind. I cannot take that money for myself anymore.
Sangeeta	:	Selfishness is certainly not in you. In fact, we are becoming selfish. According to your plan, your ashram and play school will be ready in about two years. Jeevan uncle has already become a grandfather, and you are going to become one in the next five months. In the next two to three years, our children will be ready to go to play school. We also want our children to receive a good education having emphasis on Indian tradition in your presence. So, please take it as an investment, that too for our future generations.
Jeevan	:	Wow, Child! Your ideas are truly impressive. Your level of foresight is remarkable. Such insightful thinking is a rarity in today's younger generation. It's a pleasure to have met you. I wish I had a daughter-in-law like you in my own home.
Sangeeta	:	Thank you, uncle. You can still consider me as your daughter or daughter-in-law. (Turning to Kunal) Kunal Bhaiya,

	there's no need for you to be angry with Anju bhabhi. We'll all talk to her together. Right now, it's important that our papa accepts our proposal in some way.
Jeevan	: Hey grandpa! You were already a bully. Now, you're becoming the real one. Be happy that a new guest is about to arrive at your home. Hearing such news, even a dumb person would start speaking, and a physically challenged person would start running. Don't keep things bottled up; let them burst out. Purge them out causing you trouble. Say yes to daughter-in law's proposal.
Ramesh	: (With teary eyes, looking at Sangeeta) Thank you a million times, oh God. Today, I have forgotten all my sorrows. There's no pain, no discomfort left. Ever since Inspector Sahab told me about Sangeeta, I had been eagerly awaiting this good news. I thought I would dance on hearing this news, but unfortunately, I received this news in such a state that I can't even muster a smile. Jeevan, my brother, tell these people that I don't want their money. I am enough to take care of my new generation.
Manju	: (Turning to Jeevan) *Bhai Sahab*, which wise sage did you take him to? In a moment, he completely erased all teachings the saint imparted. I should not say this, but I will. The rope has

burnt, but curls remained. What is the point of renunciation when his ego is still alive? And yes, he is not the sole owner of his property. I also have right on half of it. Ask him, Bhai Sahab, not to invest my share in his project.

Vinay : (Surprised) Mom, what's happened to you? You should be worried about dad's condition. He...

Ramesh : Hold on, son. Your mom is right. She speaks occasionally, says unpleasant things but tells the truth. (Turning towards Manju) O lucky one! Paralysis attack has twisted not just the body but also my mind. But you've straightened everything in one go.

Jeevan : Thank God, Bhabhiji has brought your wisdom back. A few minutes back, money was being offered but within next few minutes, the matter of distributing whatever was there also came up. How much more will you ponder over it? Now, just say yes, Ramesh Babu.

Ramesh : I agree to Sangeeta's proposal. We will all work selflessly for the welfare of the needy and the future generations. For two months, Jeevan and I will stay in Haridwar for health benefits. You all won't be coming with us. You will do your own duties here only. After that, in the next two to three months, our VRS will be approved. Both of us will be discharged from the hospital in couple

	of days. I have made arrangements for our stay in an *Ashram* in Haridwar.
Manju	: Brother Jeevan had already informed me about everything. Please forgive me, Vinay's dad; I hurt you even when you are in such unpleasant conditions.
Ramesh	: Yes, you hurt my feelings. Looking into all the evidence, it's clear that Jeevan supported you in this wrongdoing. Considering all the arguments, my court has reached a decision that, besides Jeevan, Manju will also accompany us for the next two months to take care of ailing Ramesh.
Manju	: Excuse me, Your Honor! This decision is incomplete. I also request the court to grant permission Sangeeta's aunt, Angoori, to come with us so that she can also have health benefits.
Ramesh	: Thank you, Manju for correcting me once more. Reforms should begin from one's own home, and my court orders that this noble work should be started with Manju's hands.

In the end, two days later, at around 6:30 in the morning, a car facing the rising sun is parked outside the hospital. Ramesh, Jeevan, Manju, and Angoori are about to leave for Haridwar in search of a new life. Ramesh has one hand on Jeevan's shoulder while in the other he is holding a crutch. He is slowly dragging his paralysed leg. The blows of nature have left both of them bias free. Similarly, Manju is having Angoori's hand on her shoulder. Although their bodies may not be supporting them anymore, the spark in their eyes is certainly the beginning of a new life. In the background, Kabir's hymn is being played. Hari bin kaun sahai man ka...

Gradually, the curtain falls.

The End

Black Eagle Books

www.blackeaglebooks.org
info@blackeaglebooks.org

Black Eagle Books, an independent publisher, was founded as a nonprofit organization in April, 2019. It is our mission to connect and engage the Indian diaspora and the world at large with the best of works of world literature published on a collaborative platform, with special emphasis on foregrounding Contemporary Classics and New Writing.

www.ingramcontent.com/pod-product-compliance
Lightning Source LLC
Chambersburg PA
CBHW060605080526
44585CB00013B/689